This book is published strictly for historical purposes.
The Naval and Military Press Ltd
expressly bears no responsibility or liability of any type,
to any first, second or third party, for any harm,
injury or loss whatsoever.

How to BOX CORRECTLY

By
JOHN J. ROMANO

Boxing Coach, Yale University 1923
Boxing Coach, Virginia Polytechnic Institute 1940
Sports Editor, Consolidated Press Assn. 1923-1938
Sports Columnist, Bell Syndicate 1934-1937
Boxing Authority, Haslin News Service 1923-1938
Boxing Editor, Collyer Publications 1941-1943

This *is* the
ONLY AUTHORIZED EDITION

Use of any part or portion of this book is severely restricted without written permission of the author.

The Naval & Military Press Ltd

Published by

The Naval & Military Press Ltd
Unit 5 Riverside, Brambleside
Bellbrook Industrial Estate
Uckfield, East Sussex
TN22 1QQ England

Tel: +44 (0)1825 749494

www.naval-military-press.com
www.nmarchive.com

In reprinting in facsimile from the original, any imperfections are inevitably reproduced and the quality may fall short of modern type and cartographic standards.

Contents

Foreword	3
Introduction	6
How to Study	6
How to Train Your Mind	7
Correct Exercising	8
Correct Diet	9
Correct Training	11
Roadwork	14
Tips on Training	15
How to Skip Rope	16
How to Bandage Your Hands	19
Punching the Light Bag	21
Fighting the Heavy Bag	23
On Guard	27
Footwork	29
The Left Jab	31
The Left Hook	33
Combining the Left Jab and Left Hook	35
The Straight Right or Right Cross	36
The One-Two	38
The Uppercut	39
Covering Up	40
Slipping the Punch	42
Shadow Boxing	43
A Further Step in Your Boxing Lessons	45
How to Hit Hard	45
The Left Jab as Used by Jackie Fields	51
Jack Dempsey and the Left Hook	53
The Combination Left Jab and Left Hook as Used by Jack Britton	55
Gene Tunney's Right Cross	57
Tony Canzoneri and the One-Two	58
Lou Nova and the Right or Left Uppercut	59
How to Second a Boxer	60
How to Judge Fights Correctly	63
Boxing Rules List 13 Fouls	65
Marquis of Queensberry Rules	65

Foreword

Boxing is a sport that has no equal for developing the keen, alert spirit of youthful America, and for making each and every youngster a pride to his nation. No other sport requires such a meager outlay of equipment and at the same time develops every function of the eye, brain and muscle. The value of boxing to the fighting man was never demonstrated to such value as in the present world conflict. The capable boxer has the advantage over his fellow-soldier and sailor in that he is better prepared to act with instant decision. The training and self discipline required of a good boxer makes him a better soldier or sailor.

This fact was emphasized in the last war when the writer was a member of the 27th Division and this series of boxing lessons was taught to small groups of officers and non-commissioned officers who in turn taught groups in their own companies. In co-operation with Staff Sergeant Major Jimmy Richards, then attached to the British Army Mission at Spartanburg, S. C., the best methods of boxing English style were incorporated with the American style so that a happy medium was obtained. Richards at the same time was the featherweight champion of the British Army and Navy and had a wealth of experience and training to qualify him for the task of incorporating the two styles. The methods used were found to be beneficial in advancing the soldiers in the use of the bayonet and proved invaluable as a training medium.

These lessons were first released through the Consolidated Press Ass'n to 144 newspapers throughout the United States and Canada. The welcome they received from readers prompted the writer to put them in book form which enjoyed so wide a response that a second edition was printed. Schools, colleges, Boy Scouts and athletic clubs subscribed to the book and it found its way to more than fifty bookshelves of colleges and physical education schools. The plain speaking and simply told lessons were easily digested so that parents and older brothers had no difficulty whatever in teaching the youths who came under their care.

The lessons deal with the essential moves of boxing, training and health care. These are told in simple words so that no puzzle is created in the young mind. More than 25,000 embryo champions have learned something from these lessons and with this in mind the BENLEE Sporting Goods Company brought out this edition so that many thousands more can benefit and prove of better value to their country.

No large group is needed to partake of the wisdom contained in these pages. One can do it alone, or better yet, induce a comrade to participate so that in a short time they will be able to test the newly acquired knowledge with the gloves on.

There is no doubt but that these lessons will prove useful. While on this subject the writer wishes to acknowledge his gratitude and respect for the fine boxing equipment the BENLEE company is making and endorses them for use by his pupils. BENLEE is a name to conjure with champions. The use of their gloves and other equipment is a by-word whenever champions fight. Their equipment is being furnished to the armed forces by government contract. This alone tells the story and to be properly equipped to fight your best it behooves you to get the best and that is BENLEE FIGHTING equipment!

JOHN J. ROMANO

New York, 1944

Introduction

At what age should a fellow begin to learn how to box for fun and for a professional career is a question in every boy's mind.

Jerry Mitchell, Sports Writer of the New York Post, asked Johnny Ray, fight manager, what was the best age at which professional boxers should begin. Here's what Ray had to say: "You've got to get a boy young to teach him real boxing—16, 17, the younger the better." We personally recommend the age of 14 or 15, for at that time a fellow's muscular and nerve senses are fully co-ordinated.

In an analysis made of the ages at which championships were won and retained, the average age for all weights was 26 years. Bantamweights averaged 24½ years. Heavyweights averaged 29½ years. This represented the average age over the years at which championships were held. Considering the fact that they were held for several years, it demonstrates the fact that championships are won in the early twenties, and that a start of some four to five years is needed to produce a well-rounded and capable fighter.

How to Study Correctly

Read slowly. Study carefully.

Sometimes one short sentence contains information that took years to gather. So be certain you clearly understand and remember everything that is said.

Be sure you understand everything in each sentence before you continue on to the next sentence.

In the beginning you will follow these lessons very closely. When you feel you have mastered the technique of the blow, there will be a tendency for you to forget the lesson. Take our advice—the human mind is quick to forget, and unless you review these lessons once a month, you are apt to lose some of the benefit. Therefore, make it a practice to read this book through the first of every month until you practically know the book by heart.

How to Train Your Mind

Self-confidence is one of the most important requirements in learning how to box. But self-confidence cannot be built up if your mind holds a lot of hidden fears and worries. Starting with the will and determination to succeed is splendid, but if you are haunted by fears and worries, you will be seriously hampered in your efforts to learn how to box or to do anything else.

Medical science, for the past 40 years, has devoted more and more attention to the relationship between a person's mental health and the condition of his body. Doctors have found that worries bring on ill health. Fear has been shown to cause the body to react as though it were sick. Unhappy feelings are the most destructive. Blood pressure, nerve tension, blood circulation and other bodily conditions are harmfully affected by a bad mental attitude. Anger, kept in your heart, burns up your nerves and your energy.

To guard yourself against getting into such a physical and mental condition, make it a habit to get everything that bothers you right off your chest—TALK IT OUT OF YOUR SYSTEM! Shoot off steam when you get angry! Don't harbor any grievances in your chest—speak your mind! If you can't speak your mind . . . if you can't "talk it off" then "box it off"—that is, use the dummy bag or the punching bag as an outlet for your grievances . . . slam hell out of the bag, and in that way get rid of your anger.

The human mind tends to exaggerate fears and to create a lot of hatreds. Invariably, when these are brought out into the open, they practically disappear.

Talk over your worries with your physician, teacher, priest or minister or any other intelligent person in whom you can put confidence. Their help will remove a lot of the ill-effects of your problems. Try to keep serene. Figure problems through instead of worrying about them aimlessly. If you cannot solve a certain problem on the day it arises, simply "put it on the shelf." Forget about it until the next day or next week whenever you plan to work it through.

Keep your interests varied. Make a lot of friends. Take part in varied activities. GET SOME RECREATION EACH DAY!

When you have developed these good habits, you will find

yourself making faster and more satisfactory progress in your boxing lessons and in every endeavor you may want to follow.

Correct Exercising

"Condition," as it is known in the boxing game, is the state of physical readiness to face an opponent in the ring. You must have this solid foundation of good health upon which to build your ability to train and box successfully.

Here are a few rules for conditioning to observe. Memorize them. Follow them religiously. Your success depends on their observance. These rules have been voted most important by coaches and trainers at the leading colleges, schools and athletic clubs throughout the country.

1. Discard all forms of tobacco, liquors and other forms of dissipation.
2. Get eight to ten hours of sleep—seven days a week. You cannot "catch up on sleep."
3. Use sufficient water, internally and externally.
4. Ventilate every room you occupy.
5. Wear light, loose and porous clothing.
6. Your street shoes should fit perfectly to keep your feet in good condition. Buy your shoes by fit. Try BOTH shoes on, walking around in them a bit to feel them out. Shoes should be ½ inch longer than your foot. The ball of your foot should rest on the widest part of the shoe. The arch and heel should fit snug. No pinching across the instep. And the front of the shoe should be broad to let your toes lie flat.
7. Secure thorough intestinal elimination daily.
8. Stand, sit and walk erect.
9. Keep teeth, gums and tongue clean.
10. Breathe deeply; take deep breathing exercises several times a day.
11. Do not allow poisons and infections to enter the body.
12. Keep serene and whole-hearted.
13. Seek out-of-door recreation.

Follow these simple rules of good health, and you will get a lot more value out of your training and boxing lessons.

Correct Diet

FOOD is important—not only to keep you alive—but to give you the necessary stamina for effective boxing. In recent years, medical science has given a lot of attention to the chemistry in food and has determined through experiments, the importance of eating various types of food.

The U. S. Department of Agriculture writes:

"First of all, did you ever figure out why you eat?

Sure, because you're hungry. But food does more than stop those hunger grumblings. It supplies the body with the stuff that makes for energy, for growth and repair of tissue, and for protection and regulation of the body functions.

For energy

Carbohydrates and fats supply food energy. The carbohydrates include starches such as macaroni, bread, and cereals, and sugars such as honey and candy. The fats include butter, cream, lard, animal fats, vegetable fats, and nut oils. They serve as fuel to make the human engine hum.

For growth and repair.

Your body needs more than energy foods to keep it going. It needs foods rich in protein for growth and repair of worn tissues. Almost all foods contain some protein, but those that have it in largest measure are meat, fish, eggs, milk and cheese, dried beans, peas, and lentils. In the quantities we eat them, bread and cereals are also a good source of protein.

For protection and regulation

That's where minerals and vitamins come in. They have been compared to the spark plugs in an engine. If you don't get enough of them, you may be able to jog along, but you won't operate smoothly, at top speed.

Calcium and phosphorus build bones and teeth. Red blood cells need iron in them to carry oxygen through the body. Without iodine for the thyroid gland, serious disturbances develop.

Foods rich in minerals are usually rich in vitamins, too. And that's good. Scientists don't know everything there is to know about vitamins yet. But they know enough to know how vital they are.

Vitamin A is needed for general good health. Night blindness is a common symptom of a deficiency. Sources of this vitamin are butter, fortified margarine, eggs, cream, milk,

U. S. NEEDS US STRONG
EAT THE BASIC 7 EVERY DAY

For health—Eat some food from each group every day

Group one—**Green and yellow vegetables,** some raw—some cooked, frozen, or canned

Group two—**Oranges, tomatoes, grapefruit** or raw cabbage or salad greens

Group three—**Potatoes and other vegetables and fruits,** raw, dried, cooked, frozen, or canned

Group four—**Milk and milk products,** fluid evaporated, dried milk, or cheese

Group five—**Meat, poultry, fish, or eggs** or dried beans, peas, nuts, or peanut butter

Group six—**Bread, flour, and cereals,** natural whole grain—or enriched or restored

Group seven—**Butter and fortified margarine** (with Vitamin A added)

In addition to the basic 7, eat any other foods you want

---

sweetpotatoes, leafy green vegetables, and certain fish liver oils.

The Vitamin B family has several important members, chief of which are thiamin or B_1, niacin, and riboflavin.

Thiamin keeps the nervous system ticking properly. It has been called the morale builder, and it was seriously lacking in the average American diet until it was put back into white bread. It is found principally in whole wheat bread and cereals, peas, beans, lentils, and nuts. Pork is also a good source.

Niacin is a factor in preventing pellagra, a disease common in the rural South, when people fail to get enough meat and milk and vegetables to eat.

Riboflavin helps the body resist disease, and is also needed for growth and vigor. Best sources of riboflavin are liver, kidney, milk, eggs, yeast, and leafy green vegetables.

Vitamin C is another "must" in the daily dietary. Oranges, lemons, grapefruit, tomatoes, cabbage, and other green leaves are best sources of this vitamin.

Vitamin D, the sunshine vitamin, is not plentiful in ordinary foods. The ultra-violet rays of the sun directly touching the skin enable the body of a human being to manufacture its own Vitamin D. People who work indoors all day, or who work in climates that do not have much sun, must get Vitamin D in foods. It can be added to milk and to bread. Cod-liver oil provides Vitamin D in concentrated form."

In addition to these suggestions, the New York City Board of Health advises:

"If you relax before meals and while you are eating, you will enjoy your food more and digest it better. Your body is over three-fourths water and it needs constant replacing. Therefore, see that you take plenty of fluids every day (but not before or during actual exercising and training). It is just as unhealthy to be too thin as to be too fat. Fruit and milk can be eaten at the same time without getting indigestion. Vegetables should be cooked in as little water as possible, and the juice should be saved instead of being poured down the sink. This is the way to prevent the loss of valuable vitamins and minerals. Adding soda to cooking water destroys vitamins. Vegetables, fruits, dark breads, and cereals are needed every day by nearly everyone to add roughage to the diet. Toast is just as fattening as fresh bread. Your body needs a real breakfast in the morning. Get up a little earlier. It pays in health. The safest rule to follow is, "Learn to eat a wide variety of foods."

For further information on food, contact your local Board of Health, the U. S. Public Health Service, and the U. S. Department of Agriculture.

Correct Training

Training should suit your individual need, for you know your own body best. If you feel out of sorts, one mile of road work will be more beneficial than five; and one round of boxing will be better than ten. Going through the motions of running or boxing when your heart or spirit is not in the work is not helpful because you get nothing out of it, and if you are feeling out of sorts there is always the danger of making your condition worse. Do not get into the habit of slackening off on your work just because you think you do not feel well. You must be honest with yourself and not be a shirker. If you are going to do a thing, do it right. You will find that the task becomes pleasant and you will get more out of doing it just for the sheer love of the feeling it produces in a healthy mind and clean body. Train conscientiously and faithfully. No champion ever attained the title by half-way measures. There is no short cut to winning. You must achieve success the right way and that is the conscientious way—the hard way.

Training should be progressive. That is, start with a few exercises and add a little each day until you are able to go through the entire program without getting too tired or taxing your physical resources. After severe exercises, stretch out flat and release all the tension of your muscles for at least five minutes.

All exercises with the exception of road work should be done at the rate of three minutes of work to one minute rest.

A full program consists of the following: Full instructions on each is given in later chapters. It is a good idea to make a written program of the things you are going to do each day.

The beginner should start road work with a walk of three miles a day. Start slowly, increasing the pace to a brisk walk or trot on the home stretch. Keep your head up and your chest out, breathing naturally and fully, with arms swinging all the time. This three-mile distance should be covered each day, but the time should be reduced two or three minutes each day until you do it within fairly fast time and not become exhausted. This means you will have to increase the distance you run to four or five miles. When you return to your room, or gymnasium, wrap yourself warmly for about ten minutes before taking a shower.

Exercise on the chest machine for about three minutes. Do not use all the plates on the machine. You should refrain from doing any other heavy exercises such as weight lifting as this will cause you to become muscle-bound.

Toss the medicine ball for about six minutes, catching the ball with your hands or arms, without allowing it to strike any other part of your body.

Skip the rope for six minutes, punch the striking bag for three minutes, shadow-box for six minutes and hit the heavy bag for six minutes.

Devote six minutes to the following exercises. Open and close your fists vigorously. This exercise will strengthen the wrist muscles and develop the grip. Strengthen the abdominal muscles by lying flat on your back, raising and lowering your legs and going through the motions of riding a bicycle. Draw your knees close to your chest and have your partner throw a medicine ball at your feet which you return by kicking straight out, making sure that you strike the ball with the soles of your feet. Develop powerful shoulders by tensing all the muscles of your arms and shoulders and swinging your arms vigorously out, down and overhead. Change the motion of your arms by raising them sideways, upward and overhead and return to the normal position by bringing them down slowly in front of you.

Finish your training period by boxing three rounds with a partner of your own weight and height. When finished, take a hot shower for three minutes. Turn off the hot water and finish up by using cold water and rubbing yourself briskly. Dry yourself with a coarse towel, paying full attention to your hair, back of the neck, crotch, and between the toes.

Sleep in a quiet, cool room. Use a small hard pillow. Breathe through your nose only.

The salvation of the athlete is deep breathing of fresh air. The boxer must learn to breathe deeply and evenly so that he will continue to do so instead of opening his mouth and gulping for air. Breathe through the nose at all times.

Stand in front of an open window before eating, fill your lungs with draughts of fresh air. Take it in slowly until you feel the air, like the mercury in a thermometer, go down to the very pit of your stomach. Draw the stomach in and expand the chest slowly and fully. Hold the breath for a short time and then permit the air to escape slowly. Continue this exercise until you feel thoroughly refreshed.

TO REDUCE WEIGHT: Omit all starchy foods such as potatoes, rice and fresh white bread from menu. One day old bread is better for you and agrees with your system. Eat plenty of vegetables. Don't drink water with your meals. Drink only on an empty stomach. Regular bowel movements are essential to weight reduction and general health. Speedy action in your gym work is the most powerful agent in weight reducing. Wear heavy clothing when exercising and doing road work.

TO GAIN WEIGHT: Include in your diet all starchy foods in addition to baked apples and bananas. Hot baths are effective. They will cause reduction but the gain thereafter will be greater than if the hot bath is omitted.

Roadwork

Taking long jogs over the roads is the best exercise there is for strengthening the legs, increasing lung power, endurance, etc. Like any other form of exercise requiring hard work this can be overdone and do more harm than good. No exercise is more harmful than overdoing road work. It is easy to bring yourself to believe that you must "tear off" five or six miles on the road. Some of your friends might have told you how much road work the champion or some other boxer in your neighborhood does every day. Remember, you must not be guided by what others do. Your body may need different work, lighter or heavier. It is far better for you to judge your own capacity than be guided by what others tell you someone else does. Pay strict heed to your own requirements and you will find you are better off than if you had made the mistake of imitating someone else.

Jog along, breathe deeply and evenly, and do not go to extremes by running until you become too tired or exhausted. Use your own good judgment when you think you have had enough and so judge each succeeding day. In this way you will find that you are able to go farther without exhaustion and better your general condition.

It is best to maintain a steady pace in your road runs. Pay strict attention to your breathing. Inhale deeply and exhale slowly and fully. By so doing you will be able to carry on longer with less effort to your breathing apparatus. Should you get a pain in the side, a "stitch," slow down and walk it off. Do not run so far that you become troubled seriously or breathe with painful effort. It is much better to stop and rest if the pain does not lessen while walking. This pain is common to the beginner, and more so when one attempts to run before he has had time to rest after a meal and thoroughly digest his food. An hour, or better still, to be on the safe side, two hours should elapse before attempting any strenuous exercises such as running.

A good method to "sharpen" the wind and enable you to bring your reserve forces into play, (the condition the athlete calls his "second wind") is to measure off a distance of 100 yards, sprint that distance, and then walk 200 yards. This will enable you to regain your measured, steady breathing before sprinting another 100 yards. As advised before, you are the best judge of your ability and can rate yourself so as to be sure and not overdo it. Be moderate in your work. It is better to finish up with something in reserve.

Warm clothing should be worn on your road runs. A heavy pair of shoes should always be worn. Should you step on a stone while using a light pair of shoes you are apt to turn your ankle, suffer a stone bruise or tear a ligament. Another benefit you will derive from using heavy shoes is that you will be accustomed to the heavier weight and when you step into a gymnasium and use light boxing shoes you will scarcely notice the weight, making you that much faster afoot.

Always use an elastic supporter, while on the road. This is a precaution against strains while running.

Tips on Training

You often hear the expression, "He left his fight in the gym," or "He left his fight on the road." In most cases this is true because the boxer overdid his work, worked too hard in the gym or burnt up too much energy by lengthy road runs. MODERATION SHOULD BE FOLLOWED IN ALL FORMS OF EXERCISING.

Attempting to build up too quickly by arduous work when you do not feel right and "pushing" yourself just because you had planned to run or jog two miles when one mile would have accomplished better results, is bad.

When you have to make weight, something a young boxer should never do because it proves faulty and sometimes shortens your career as a boxer, it may become necessary for you to wear an extra shirt or sweat shirt and in some rare cases RUBBER PANTS. Never a RUBBER SHIRT! You can afford to boil excess fat off the hips and buttocks but never from the upper portion of the body where you naturally want to carry weight to add power to your blows. Then again the use of a rubber shirt is frowned upon by medical authorities and serious illness may result by using such an extreme to take off weight.

Another good thing to do is carry two small rubber balls, one in each palm of the hand, and squeeze them as you walk, trot or run. This seemingly meaningless little exercise has been found to be a valuable aid in strengthening the small muscles of the fingers and the wrist.

How to Skip Rope

Skipping the rope is a valuable aid in developing speedy footwork and the proper use of the feet without undue effort. Instinctive moves of the feet are bettered and perfected by the rhythm and sustained effort of the boxer who uses this exercise for that purpose.

The exercise also limbers up the muscles of the biceps, wrists and shoulders. The light movement makes the muscles supple and responsive to the coordination of the mind and movements of the legs.

When skipping the rope you must always be on your toes. Throw the rope back over your head and rise on your toes. Bring the rope forward and as it passes before your eyes raise both feet lightly to permit the rope to pass under them. Your hands should describe a revolving motion as you do this. In so doing you will be able to continue the revolution of the rope for as long as you are able to "skip" the rope as it passes beneath your feet.

It is easier to learn how to skip the rope by lifting both feet in unison. This will enable you to become accustomed to the exercise without getting too puzzled and getting your feet mixed up. After you have learned to get over being clumsy you will be able to use the feet singly and go through the motions of riding a stationary bicycle and permitting the rope to pass under your feet without getting tripped.

Now try to skip with one foot in front of the other. Place the left foot forward so that the heel is on a line with the toe of the right foot. Repeat the exercise, turning the rope and raising the feet as the rope is descending. Continue this move until you have mastered it. Then reverse the movement, right foot forward and left foot to the rear. After you have learned this move you must try to reverse the movement of the feet every time the rope descends. That is, first the right foot is forward as the rope descends and when the rope reaches the top of the arc and begins to descend put your left foot forward and bring the right foot back and permit the rope to pass underneath. This will be puzzling at first. It is best to learn this move without using the rope. Interchange the movements of the feet by stepping out with the right foot forward and then bring it back and the left foot forward. This will give you an idea what to do with the feet when you turn the rope. Practise foot movement because it will teach you how to move the feet easily and without much attention. That is, you will learn how to use your feet quickly and gracefully without seeming to think about what you are doing.

As noted before, you cannot expect to start right off and skip the rope. Like all moves in boxing or training it requires practise and you must be careful and patient. Practise slowly and you will speed up as you learn the trick of the exercise. You will soon learn how to skip the rope at a rate of about 120 turns to the minute.

Skip three minutes to a round. Rest one minute between rounds. Five or six rounds is generally sufficient for a beginner. When the weather prevents you from doing road work you can make up for it by adding a few extra rounds for good measure.

These Fighting Words from Fighting Leaders to their Fighting Men is Good Advice to Boxers, too:

"Hit hard ... hit fast ... hit often."
—ADMIRAL HALSEY

"Get 'em off balance ... don't let 'em get set ... and keep on punching."—MAJOR-GENERAL GILLEM

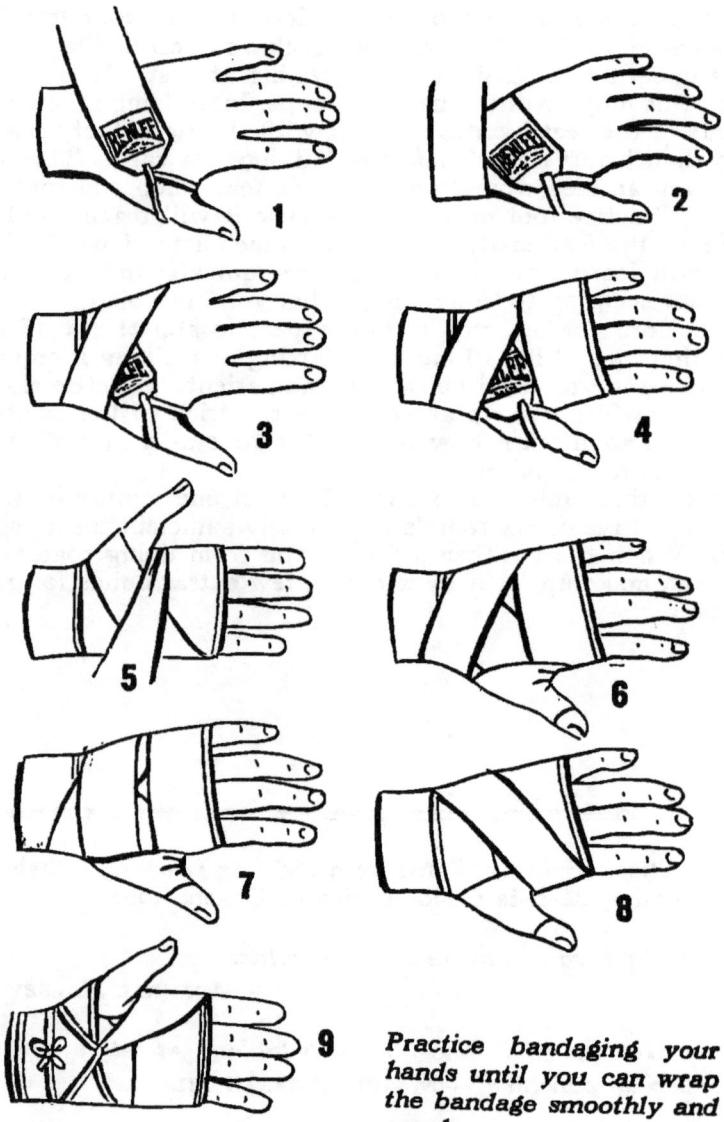

Practice bandaging your hands until you can wrap the bandage smoothly and evenly.

How to Bandage Your Hands

Bandaging the hands properly is essential to a boxer because an improperly bandaged hand is worse than no taping at all. It is far better for a boxer to do without the protective wrappings than its is to enter a bout with poorly taped hands.

In training, use wool or cotton wrappings. These will not only save the hands from damage when striking a hard object, but will also act as a shock absorber and save the small bones of the hands from fractures that may occur from the heavy poundings you will subject them to.

Put the thumb through the loop at one end of the bandage flat up over and around the wrist. Take several turns around the wrist and then bring it down across the hand and around the four knuckles. Wind it around so that the surface of the bandage is flat on the hand and does not twist and snarl unevenly. Close the hand and open it several times during the bandaging process. This will prevent the wrappings from becoming too tight and prevent you from closing your fist after the job is completed. You will save considerable annoyance and time, if you remember this because so many do the job improperly and have to take off the bandage and rewind it.

Practise tying the bandage until you feel that it lays snug on the hand and takes up the jar when you strike a blow against the heavy or light bag. The sharp, even impact tells you that the hand is properly bandaged, that you have taken the necessary measures to guard against injury, and that the job is well done.

Never bring the bandage between the fingers of the hand. This makes a lump and may appear to satisfy the newcomer, but by so doing he spreads the little bones in his hands and defeats the purpose of bandaging.

See pages 5 and 68 for important announcements

How to Box Correctly

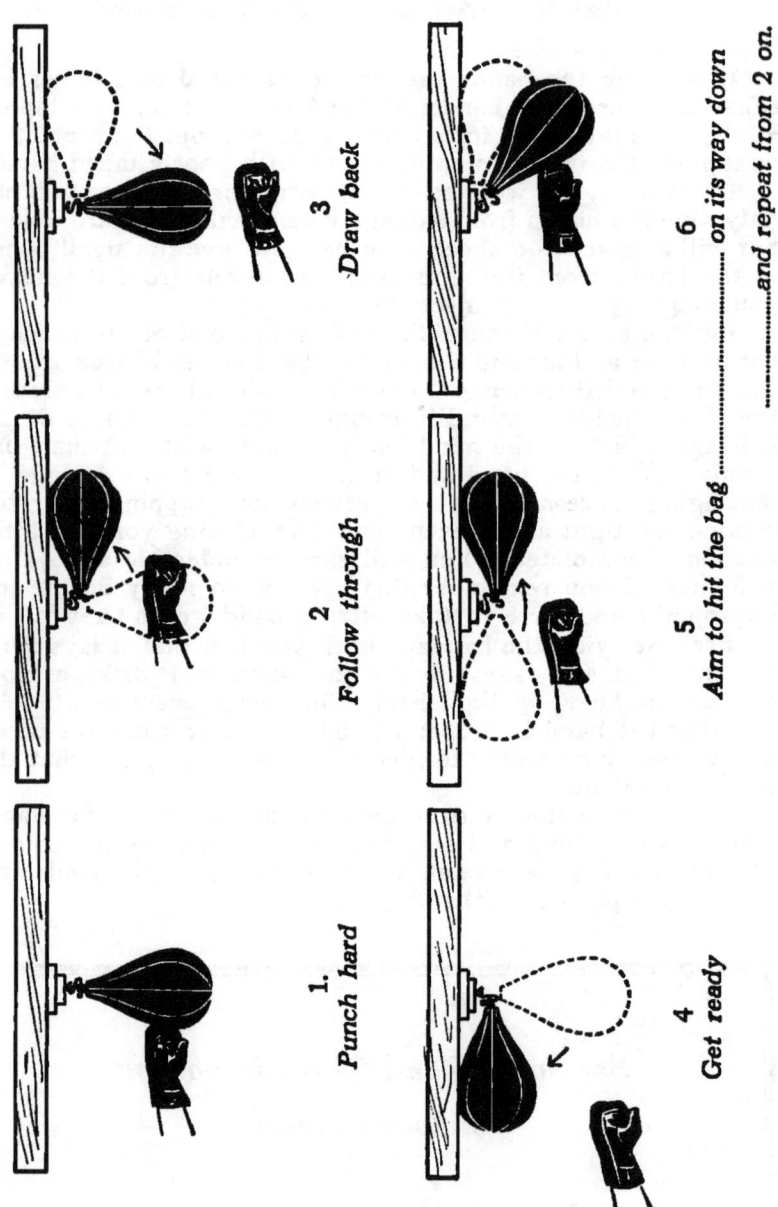

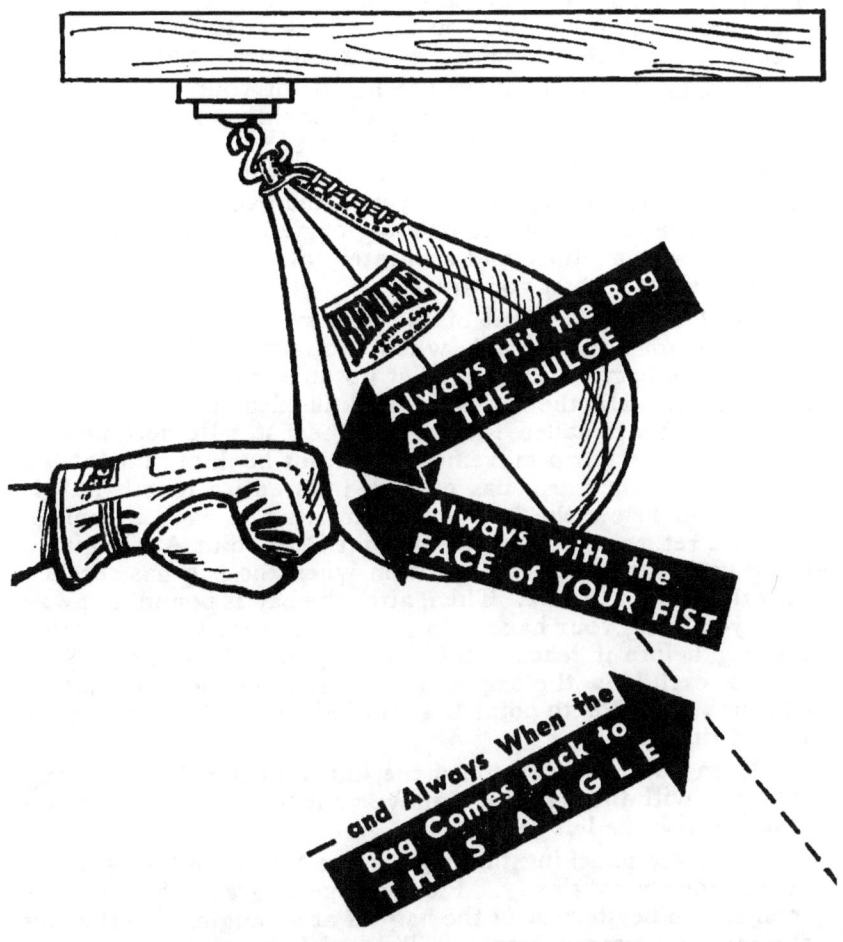

Punching the Light Bag

Punching the light bag is an essential part of your training program for it helps you develop blows to the head, and trains your eyes to measure a bobbing target accurately. In addition, it helps develop the muscles of the arms, shoulders, neck, wrist and legs. It makes the muscles flexible, promotes deep breathing and is a pleasing, enjoyable form of exercise.

Before taking your stand in front of the bag, bear in mind

that you must start slowly and continue slowly until you become proficient, otherwise you cannot expect to gain the speed needed to make the exercise pleasing and beneficial.

The bag should be about the height of your chin, so that you can hit straight out instead of looping your blows and bringing them up to meet the ball. After you have learned to hit straight out will be time enough to raise or lower the bag so that you can hit higher or lower at the bag. The idea is to train the eye to level on the bobbing bag and train the muscles to strike out forcefully and accurately at an opponent who is taller or shorter than you are.

Stand directly in front of the bag, sway your body to the left until your right hand, when brought up, is directly in front of the bag. Bring your fist up and send it into the bag at the bulge. Hit the bag with the knuckles and joints of the fingers. This is called the face of the fist. Be certain that this is a straight arm movement. Do not hook or chop at the bag. When your arm has extended its entire length pull it back again below the bag and then bring it back in unison with the return of the bag from point B to point A. Begin to bring your hand back into position when the bag has reached the other end of the arc. Then, after the bag is bounding away from you bring your hand into position so that you will strike the bag before it reaches the lowest point of the arc. Note that for each blow the bag strikes point B, bounds to point A, and then rebounds to point B again before you hit the bag the second time.

When you have developed the knack of punching the bag correctly with the right hand move your body to the right and practise with the left hand.

If you are punching the bag for the first time follow these instructions very slowly. Pick up speed gradually. But as soon as you begin to send the bag off at an angle, stop the bag and start over again, slower. Then pick up speed as you get the bag rebounding true.

You cannot expect to judge the rebound of the ball at the start. The elusiveness of the rebound will disconcert and possibly discourage you. Keep trying and follow directions and you will soon get the hang of it. You will have to learn how to hit it squarely, how much force to put behind the blow, and to keep the hands elevated so that you will not have to bring them up too great a distance to meet the ball on the rebound.

The quickest way to learn how to punch the bag is to remember you must start slowly and keep it up until you gain confidence and you will begin to pick up speed without knowing it. If you attempt to punch the bag at a rapid pace too early you will find that you will be bringing your hand all the way up to the top of the platform and chopping down with the middle joints of the fingers instead of hitting with the "face" of the fist. This is to be avoided for not only does it present the possibility of hitting your hands against the platform, but it also results in a useless swing that is never used in boxing. Then, too, you will be developing the wrong way of bag punching that will take a long time to correct.

Don't try fancy bag punching because you will be learning a lot of punches that are not to be used in boxing. Instruction books on bag punching show how to hit the bag from side to side, with the side of your fist, with your elbows and wrists, and other fancy ways. These blows are all right for fellows who want to use the bag only for exercising. But if you were to get in the habit of using these fancy punches, you would soon find yourself automatically using wrong punches while boxing, and these may result in injury to your hand or in foul blows.

Use the bag only for practicing jabs, one-two and hooks. Do not punch the bag with any blow you do not use in actual fighting.

Fighting the Heavy Bag

Don't box another fellow until you have learned how to box and defend yourself properly. If you don't have this basic knowledge you run the needless risk of injury. Be certain you have every blow under control before you put the gloves on with somebody else.

The heavy bag is perfect for learning how to deliver the various blows. However, before training with the heavy bag, first learn the technique of each blow as given in the next part of the book. Practice these blows in the air first. Then, when you believe you have them under control, use the heavy bag for perfecting each punch.

The light bag is best suited for light, speedy accurate hitting. The matter of proper hitting, getting the full force behind the blow without danger of breaking one of the many small bones in the hands is ever present. That is where the heavy training bag comes in.

Hang the bag so that the bottom is on the level with your hips. This will give you a target to hit at without the tendency to hit lower than the belt or waist-line. Assume the position "on guard" and strike out as though you were facing an opponent. You will note from the "feel" of the fist striking the resilient object in front of you whether you are hitting correctly and whether or not you are getting the maximum power behind the blow. A turn of the wrist, one knuckle hitting harder than the other, or the thumb striking the bag will tell you that you are hitting wrong. You can easily correct this fault by punching slower and observing how you are striking, what is wrong, and what you should do to execute the move properly.

Jab at the bag as you would an opponent. Cross your right with all the power you can get behind the blow and continue this move until you can deliver the two blows with the least loss of time between the jab and following right cross. REMEMBER TO HIT OUT STRAIGHT ALL THE TIME! LEARNING TO HOOK PROPERLY: It is best to practice hooking your blows from a standing position. Stand flat-footed and arch your blows so that you can deliver the punches with a shortened arc. This will tend to stop you from bringing the fist back, which is swinging, and the shortened hook will enable you to get more power behind the punch. Alternate, using both hands in this exercise. Many boxers have been known to concentrate on one blow at a time so that they become nearly perfect in the use of the blow. There is nothing really wrong in perfecting either the right or left hook. But it is preferable to be able to use either hand with equal facility. Do not place too much reliance on one blow. Be fair to yourself and practice diligently with both the right and left hand.

After you have learned how to hit the bag while it is stationary it is a good idea to give the bag a slight push to set it swinging slowly. Do not strike at the bag while it is coming to you. Wait until it has started to swing away and then hook sharply, with the right or left, in the direction of the swing of the bag. This is valuable practice as it accustoms you to hitting the side or short sides of an opponent who turns from a blow.

The heavy bag is also used to develop the "tattoo," or rapid hitting to the body. This is called "infighting" and is a commendable trait in the American style of boxing. Bring your right foot up so that it is on a line with the left. Crouch slightly forward and bring both hands upward in short, sharp blows into the bag. The bag will give. Press forward a little more and continue hitting away with both hands. Repeat this move from time to time imagining you have an opponent before you who is fighting in close quarters. Try to visualize your opponent coming in or backing away and "fight" the bag as you would your opponent. In other words, if the bag is stationary, you must figure your opponent is close up and ready to go into action. Step up to the bag as though to meet

"ON GUARD" POSITION

This picture points out the most important elements in taking the On Guard position. Study these carefully. Then read the rest of the instructions under "On Guard" on the next three pages.

your opponent, punch away with both hands and when the bag gives way you assume that your opponent is backing away from your attack. Step closer and continue punching away with both hands. Assume that your opponent is holding. Back away and quickly return to the attack with both hands. This will enable you to get more force behind your blows and teach you to stay in close so that your opponent's blows are robbed of their force.

You can also use the heavy bag for sparring. Step nimbly around the suspended object, jab lightly, step away and jab again, following up these moves with a sharply driven right cross. Jab and hook with the left. The jab should be light so that you bring it back quickly and get leverage behind the shortened arc of your swing—the hook. Feint low at the bag and bring the punch upward to the level of your face. The combination jab and hook is a deceptive duo of blows and has a good chance of landing if you use it to befuddle your opponent into lowering his guard.

Work on the heavy bag should be timed into rounds. Three minutes of exercise and one minute of rest is sufficient. Three or four rounds for each session is enough for the beginner.

On Guard

Boxing, like any other study, must be learned from the bottom up. The feet play an important part in the career of a boxer, and boxing bouts are won or lost by the proper or improper movements of the feet. The proper stance places you in a position so that you will be solid, firm and able to deliver a solid blow with the proper leg leverage and yet not be knocked off balance.

Using the position "on guard" bring your left foot forward a pace, turning the toes so that they point slightly to the right. The right foot should be back about 18 inches, the heel almost on a line with the left, and the toes pointing to the right.

To prove that this is your proper position,

For the fellow with a short reach, and not fast on his feet, this "crouch" style of the On-Guard position is recommended.

that you are at ease, try this exercise. Raise yourself on the balls of your feet and go down, using a springy motion, several times. Sway from side to side and then try bending forward again without moving your feet. If you can do this without losing your balance and feel that you have perfect control of your body, you are standing correctly.

Practice this exercise frequently so that you can better learn the proper distance which should separate your feet. This will cause you to spring instantly on guard, be balanced and on the alert to take the offensive or assume the defensive.

Here is another exercise. Bend backward and forward from the hips and bend the knees at the same time to conform with the move. This is what is called "weaving." In later lessons, or when you become adept in boxing, you will learn to "roll" with a punch, thereby breaking the force of the blow or get out of range without taking a backward step.

Note carefully the position of the THUMB when the fist is made.

Learn to move around easily on the balls of the feet. A gliding motion requires less effort than stepping around. You will be surprised how much faster and with less effort and with more grace you can glide than step around.

The left hand should be closed, but not too tightly because the muscles of the fingers will become strained and cause them to open when you deliver a blow. When making a fist, do not extend the thumb beyond the knuckles. Instead, fold the thumb across the fingers. This will keep it from getting hurt when your fist strikes.

Put your left hand half-way out so that the fist is on a line with your opponent's jaw. The elbow should be slightly crooked downward. You can then deliver a jab or a hook without having to pull the hand back and thus give your opponent a chance to know what to expect.

Crooking the elbow makes for greater flexibility. It permits you to draw your hand back quickly should you be called upon to defend yourself against a countering blow.

The right hand should be brought back, partly open, so that the elbow points directly to the floor. This method of guarding the right side, both face and body, permits you to use the right both offensively and defensively. If a blow is directed to your body, you can without waste of time and effort, move your elbow toward the body to ward it off or break the force of the blow. The gloved right fist, being high, is in position to strike out or fend off a blow.

Bend your knees slightly. This permits you to execute your moves more naturally.

Drop your chin in the hollow formed by the collar-bone and shoulder. If your vision is not clear, hunch your shoulder a little more until you can see without effort, being careful to keep your chin covered as much as you can.

Footwork

Foot work plays an important part in boxing. The force of a blow will be lessened by a short move in or out, as the case may be, and you will be in position to counter before your opponent recovers.

Foot work does not mean jumping and hopping around. So many beginners have an idea that dancing, hopping away and around the ring is clever foot work. Nothing is further from the truth. Running away counts against you. Hopping around puts you off balance and the slightest blow will upset you. There must be a reason behind every move. There is no necessity of useless moving about, wasting strength and energy just to be doing something.

By all means learn how to move around on the balls of the feet. Some boxers find it expedient to bend back and forth from the hips, keeping the head bobbing around. A moving target is more difficult to hit. A slight turn of the head, either way, prevents the blow from landing solidly. Others find it better suited to their natural actions to weave the head and body. This also acts to break the force of the blow.

These moves come under the heading of foot work in that they perform the same purpose of stepping out of range of a blow.

If you must move around to make your opponent box as you want him to, at a disadvantage from his best style of boxing, always move in the opposite direction of his hardest and best blow. Suppose your are boxing an opponent who hits hard with his right. The thing for you to do is to move in a circle towards his left. By doing this you are able to break the force of the wallop by going away with it, turning your shoulder to the blow or putting out your left to fend it off.

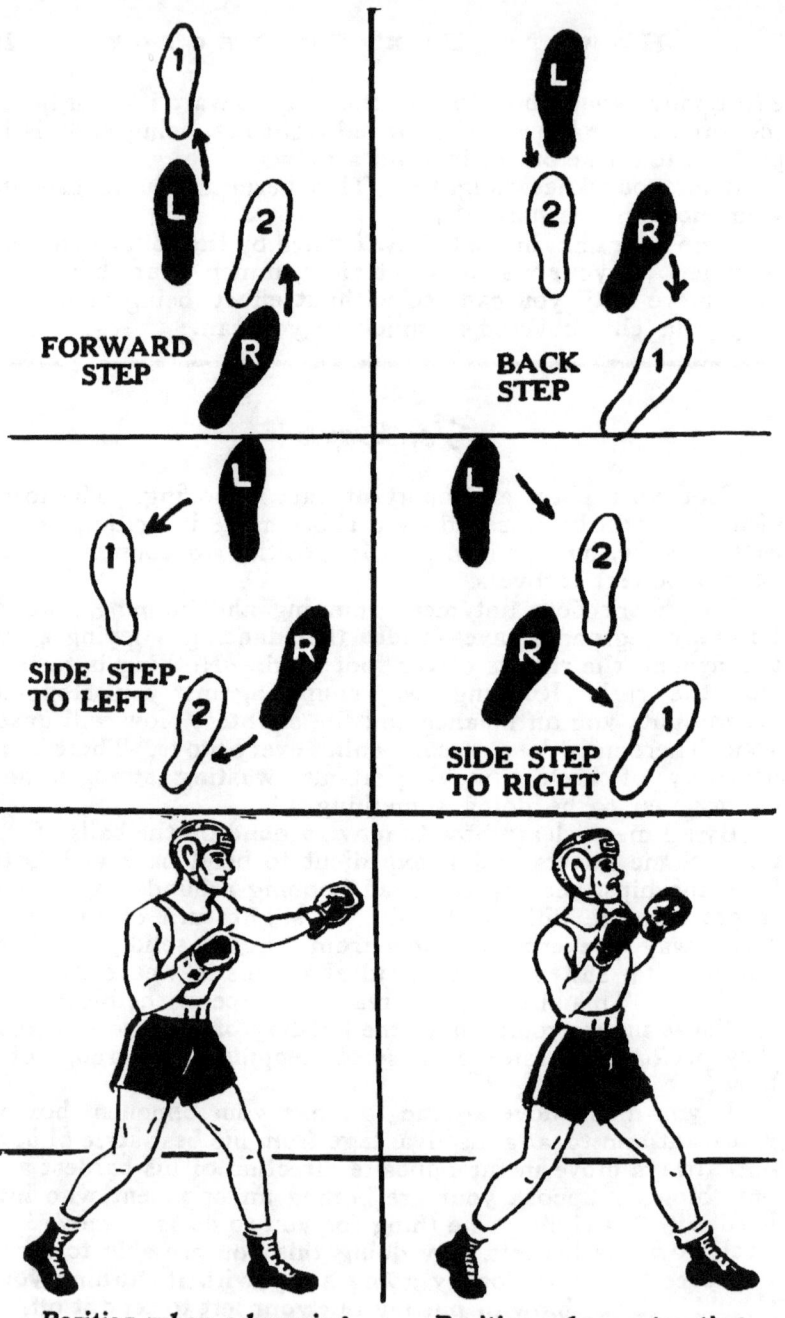

The same move works in the opposite direction when you are boxing an opponent who stands off with his right hand and foot forward. He is what is called a "south paw."

Don't show your disregard of your opponent by refusing to back away. It is a good policy to back away at times. It is better to move out of range of damaging blows when you are unprepared. Also, by backing away you can lead your opponent into thinking you are afraid of the issue. This will cause him to become over-confident, possibly swing wildly to reach you or fall short with his blows. That is the opportunity you seek or make for yourself. You can hit out with either hand in retaliation.

The purpose of foot work is to lead your opponent into false leads and present a deceptive mark for him to hit at; and more than anything else, to carry you out of danger when you are hurt or flustered.

Don't cross your feet. Move around sure footed, gracefully, with the object of being in position to defend yourself or to strike out swiftly.

The Left Jab

Note how the fist turns with the delivery of the blow. The knuckles face UP when the blow is struck.

The left jab is really a sharp thrust. It is not a knockout blow. It is used to score points, disconcert an opponent, draw his guard down or make a false move and thus create an opening for a heavier blow such as a right cross or left hook.

The value of the jab cannot be over-emphasized. Proficient use of the jab is a valuable asset to all boxers. Many contests are won by the skillful use of the jab.

From the position "on guard," shoot your left fist, straight out, aiming for the jaw or mouth, turning the body slightly to get added reach and force to the blow. As you thrust out with your left, raise your right hand slightly to conform with the move.

Bring the hand back smartly for another jab or to guard against a countering blow.

One thing you must always remember. Don't permit your right hand to drop as you step in to jab. This will leave your jaw exposed.

"Feint" your opponent into leaving an opening before you jab. "Feinting" is an incompleted jab. This is how it is done. Bend forward as you paw out the left describing a downward, circular motion. When you think you can strike cleanly, arrest the circular motion and thrust out straight.

Should your opponent jab while you are "feinting," turn the palm of your right hand out to touch his glove and push it away from you. Pull your head back as you do this in case you miss his glove. Thus you will lessen the force of the blow or cause it to fall short.

Don't attempt to jab from a stationary position unless it is to stave off a rush. You can always beat a swinging blow by stepping in smartly with a stiff jab.

As you feint, slide your left foot forward at the same time bringing up the right so that too much distance does not separate the feet. This is important. If you don't bring up the right foot you will be off balance and easily pushed or knocked off your feet.

Jab as you come within arm's length. This is called "judging distance."

Be careful not to over-reach. Don't be afraid to step in or your blow will fall short of the mark. This will leave you open to body-blows, uppercuts or hooks.

Don't jab with the open glove. Close your fist so that the knuckles hit solidly.

Don't be afraid to strike out sharply, repeatedly, when your opponent comes at you with both hands swinging. Your jabs will beat the other fellow's blows and force him to clinch.

Again, don't raise your head as you jab. When the left is extended, make sure the chin is protected by the hunch of your shoulder. This will keep your head down.

Don't jab when you are going away unless your opponent is rushing you.

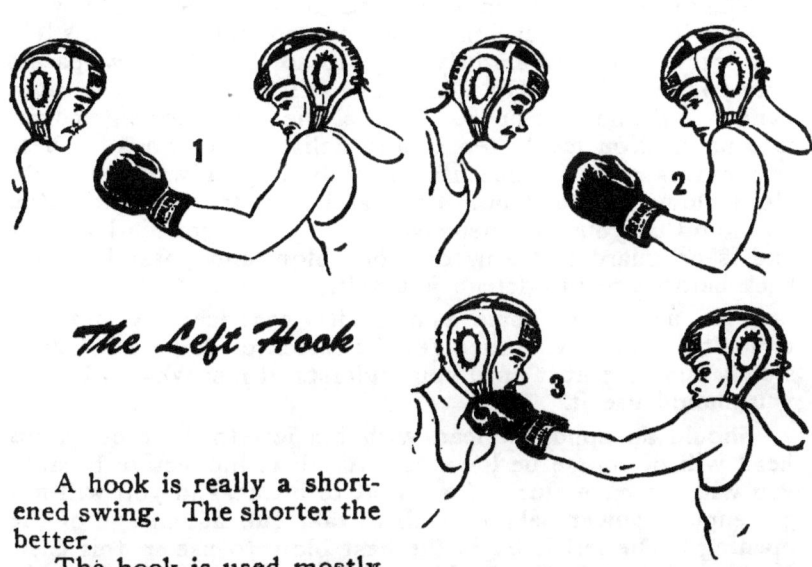

The Left Hook

A hook is really a shortened swing. The shorter the better.

The hook is used mostly as a countering blow. It can be put to effective use at long range, that is, if you step in with it and beat your opponent to the punch. It is better if you concentrate on the left hook at short range. At long range, there is a tendency to pull the arm back to get more force behind it and thus widen the arc of the swing. You must be on your guard against swinging. You will fall into the habit of swinging if you try to hook at long range and try to put too much behind the punch.

The method of delivering the hook is: Assume the position "on guard." Drop your elbow slightly and propel the fist upward and in sideways to your opponent's jaw so that it describes an arc. Don't lift your elbow as you deliver the blow. If you bring the elbow on a level with the fist, you will strike with the thumb or the first knuckle of the hand. The face of the fist, the four knuckles, must land fully to get the desired effect. Then you will know that you are executing the move properly.

As you practise it and become used to the move, you will raise your left heel slightly and give the hip an upward twist. This is called "leg leverage." Getting the heel and hip motion in perfect unison with the motion of the fist will cause you to add a little snap to the wrist as you land the blow. This little snap adds to the force and speed of the blow.

The use of the left hook requires courage, especially when you use it as a counter. Suppose your opponent leads his left, you parry it or bend slightly forward so that the blow passes over your shoulder. His next move will invariably be a right hander to the head or body. That is when your courage comes into play. You must step in and deliver your hook. These two moves must be executed rapidly if you wish to get a clean blow in. Don't pull away and then try to hook. You will find that your opponent has already brought his left back and is on guard to throw off your blow and possibly strike back before you can defend yourself.

This move will come easier with practice. It is not a difficult one after you once get the knack of doing it. Try it slowly and keep at it until you understand just why and when you should use it.

Should an opponent lead with his left to your body, his head will of course be lowered. A jab is ineffective because you will not have much of a target to hit at, and you will not get enough power behind a jab to take full advantage of the opening. The left hook is the best blow to use in this case. You have a better chance of hitting him on the jaw and knocking him off balance and into position for a right hander.

Here is another case. Your opponent over-reaches with a left jab and he starts a swing for the head. The proper blow is a left hook to the body.

The left hook to the body, when properly used, is one of the most punishing blows in the whole category. Hitting a man to the wind and heart slows him up, causes him to lower his guard and gives you a better chance to strike at the face and jaw.

This is a blow that should be practised on the heavy bag. It is worth a little extra practise as it is a bit more complicated than the jab. Note particularly whether you get any leverage behind the blow, the leg and hip, and whether you land solidly. You will notice that the more you shorten the arc the fist describes, the harder you will land.

Combining the Left Jab and Left Hook

Combining two moves requires instinctive thought and movement. The effectiveness of the combination lies in the delivery of the blows without loss of time or motion between one and the other.

You jab at your opponent. You note that he does not raise his right quick enough to ward off the thrust. Try your jab again and if you notice that his right does not come up quickly, draw your hand back just a little and drive in with a left hook.

Or, your opponent leads to the body. You fend the blow or knock it down with your right. Step in smartly with a jab. This will lift your opponent's head, because he has in most cases already started his right, and you hook for the open target.

Suppose you are boxing a fellow who throws your leads to his left, across his body. Sooner or later that fellow will make this move, passing his hand across his face, even though you do not fully extend your arm. (In a previous lesson you were told this move is called a "feint") Using the same motion, only depressing the elbow, you can put over a hook before he has time to bring back his right to parry the blow.

Avoid using your guarding hand, the right, in meaningless motions. That is, keep it steady until you wish to use it to fend a blow or deliver one.

When you are boxing an opponent who weaves (a swaying motion of the hands and body) strike out with a light jab as his head comes in front of you and drop the elbow so that your hooking fist meets the jaw as the head returns to the place it was when you jabbed. This is called "timing."

As noted before, the effect of the hook is more pronounced when your opponent is coming in to you. In combination with the jab, the hook is not a counter blow. It is a "follow up" punch because the jab opens the way for its delivery.

There are many more cases when the jab and the hook can be used as one move. As you practise more, by boxing with an opponent, you will readily detect openings or chances to use either the hook or jab, or both in combination with each other.

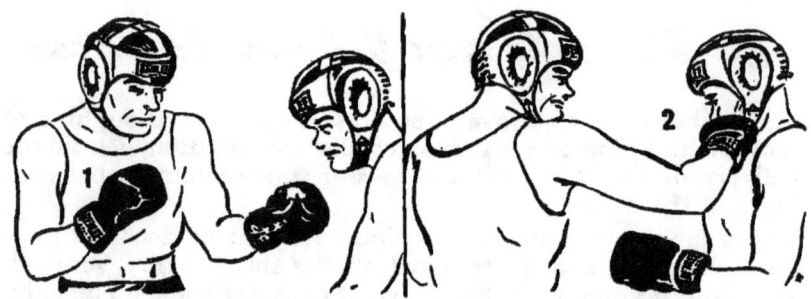

The Straight Right or Right Cross

One of the cardinal rules for a boxer to remember is: Never lead with your right! The distance is too great for the blow to travel and leaves you wide open for a countering blow.

All through these lessons you have been taught to hit straight out.

The straight right hand blow usually follows a left lead. As in delivering the hook, try to get that little lift of the hip and shoulder as you drive your fist out. This is done by raising your elbow slightly as you start the punch and bringing the body forward with the move. This is similar to the "follow through" motion the golfer gives the body the instant the club strikes the ball.

The fingers of the hand (fist) should be parallel with the floor as you strike, so that the knuckles, all four of them, land.

Unless your opponent is far enough away so that the arm is fully extended when you land the blow, you will not get enough power behind it to make it fully effective. That is one reason why you should not attempt to land the right when your opponent is set for the blow. He can knock it down or aside with his left and counter with a left hook. Or, he will bob his head under the blow and smash you solidly with a body blow.

The straight right to the body

When you use the straight right, remember to bring your left back quickly so that the elbow is pointing downward and the left is protecting the jaw. Should you neglect to do this and leave the jaw exposed, your opponent can beat you to the punch with his own right, a matter of having a faster right. Remember the straightest, fastest blow lands first.

Beating a man to the punch is always the best way of landing with terrific force. The impact of a fist landing on a body moving forward is always greater.

Using the right to the body, drop your glove as you step in and drive in short and straight, remembering to keep your left hand high as a guard. This blow is mostly used to beat the left jab, after you have learned to time the blow by lowering the head and letting it go over your shoulder. The right to the body is very effective at close quarters. It is a solid damaging blow.

To the observer, the short punches to the body do not look so good or spectacular as the long ones to the head. You are not concerned with the impressions of the spectators. Hitting sharply to the wind and body are bound to have an effect on the defensive work of your opponent. It puts him on the defensive and you have less to worry about as you move around looking for an opening.

During your boxing practise you will sometimes find that you cannot land cleanly with your right. It may be that your opponent, rightly enough, keeps his chin lowered so that the hunch of the shoulder protects it. In such a case be careful of too promiscuous use of the right. You may break up your hands or stave in the knuckles by landing on the head.

One way of reaching your opponent's jaw is to loop your punch. That is, send your blow high so that it describes an upward arc and curves down so that it lands on the small portion of the exposed jaw.

"Boxing and Wrestling develop endurance, agility, and strength, and are important factors in the development of confidence, courage, and self-control."—*Basic Field Manual, Physical Training (F.M. 21-20) U. S. Army.*

"Boxing helps to develop an aggressive combative spirit, self-reliance, stamina and courage."—*Shipmate Magazine, "The Eyes and Ears of the Navy."*

38 HOW TO BOX CORRECTLY

The One-Two

The "one-two" punch is a combination of the left jab and the straight right. Some boxers, instead of using a straight, thrust-like left, hit with the back of the left hand and follow through with a straight right. The left jab is better and more to be desired as it is faster. The proper execution of this move depends on the speed of the following right hand punch. As in all combinations of blows, there should be no hesitation between the blows. They should be combined so that the two moves are executed in unison.

Don't put too much force behind the left jab. If you do, you will drive your opponent's head back out of the range and the right will fall short of the mark.

The left is used as a cover, to camouflage the following-up blow.

This is the way it should be practised. Assume the position of "on guard." The right elbow should be slightly raised. This releases the tension of the muscles which ordinarily sets in when the arm is raised. Paw out your left so that your opponent is fooled into thinking it a meaningless blow. Keep it high so that the vision of your opponent is covered and then drive through with a straight right.

The chances of landing the one-two with any degree of success depends on the amount of deception you can bring into play with the leading left. By this is meant, how much you have been able to fool your opponent into dropping his guard or becoming careless by feinting him to disguise what you mean to do. Or by putting over a stiff left jab when the occasion warrants or when you have flustered your man by a mixture of blows.

Effective use of the one-two punch paves the way for a knockout blow. If you can catch your man solidly with a straight right to the body after delivering the one-two, you will bring his guard down and switch back to the head quickly.

Don't attempt to one-two your opponent when he is backing away from you. You will fall short of your mark and be wide open for a countering hook or straight punch to the head or body. Remember this when your opponent tries the one-two punch on you. Step back out of range and come right back driving both hands for the body.

One way to break up the one-two punch is to duck your head under the left lead so that the following right will go harmlessly over your shoulder, then punch away at the exposed body in front of you. This move calls for quick thinking and instant action.

When you have learned to uppercut, you will find this blow useful in countering an incomplete one-two punch.

Remember it is easier to reach the body with solid blows than it is to hit the rolling, bobbing head. The body offers a larger, more stationary target.

The Uppercut

The right or left uppercut is an inverted hook. That is, the elbow and fist are driven upward instead of describing a looping arc.

Particular attention should be paid to the method of delivery, especially how the fist strikes the jaw or body. The fingers of the hand used to strike the blow should face your body so that all the knuckles strike the object on landing.

The uppercut, like the hook, requires courage on the part of the boxer using it. The blow is most effective when you are moving in to counter an over-reaching jab or swing. By constantly practising the blow, you will learn to act quickly in deciding whether the situation calls for an uppercut or a hook. Usually the uppercut gets the preference when your opponent's blows are aimed for the head, as his body will be left wide open.

Don't try to uppercut at long range. This is nothing more than an upward swing, easily knocked down and leaves you in danger of being hit with a cross counter with the right.

A right or left uppercut is effective when you are facing an opponent who bores in with lowered head using both hands to punch the body. By covering up until you get in close, you can break up your opponent's attack with uppercuts, both hands, to the head. It would do well to keep this in mind when you elect to use both hands to the body or fall short with a jab or one-two punch. A right or left uppercut will find the way to your jaw.

The right uppercut from a crouch position.

A swinger is an easy mark for an uppercut. By stepping inside of the swing you can bring either hand up to the jaw. It is a jarring, lifting blow.

A good point to remember when using the uppercut is to have the other hand ready to block or parry a countering blow. Don't drop your guard as you start the uppercut. By this is meant, don't drop both hands as if undecided which to use for the blow.

Covering Up

Covering up is an art in itself. The boxer who can cover up and prevent his opponent from striking a damaging blow has the upper hand. A good defensive boxer is a rarity. So many try to do all the punching. It is far better to learn how to guard properly by covering the jaw and body. You are then less apt to be hit with a hard blow. Avoiding punishment is one of the chief reasons everyone should learn to box.

Although it is poor policy to cross the hands over the head or body, there are times when it is necessary. The reason the hands should not cross themselves is that you have curtailed one of their uses—the offense. The hands should be in position to guard and hit at the same time. If you cross your hands you are blocking all right, but you will have to draw them back to hit. For instance, if you throw a jab to your left side, you will have to bring your own hand back all the way before you can hit with it. That is why you have been taught to fend off a lead or swing by throwing it away from you. By doing this your own hand will be in position to strike out without loss of time and motion. The same advice holds good when you use the left to block a swing. If you raise the shoulder and bring the right hand over to cover the jaw, the right is confined to that one move. Instead, raise the left and catch the swing on the glove or forearm and continue the move by converting it into a hook. You will get the hang of this by practising the move.

There may be times when you are being punished severely about the head and body. It is advisable to cross the hands over the punished parts. This will permit you to escape a certain amount of punishment, get your wits together, and shake off the effects of damaging blows.

Sometimes this defense is used as a subterfuge to draw your opponent into believing you are badly hurt so that he wastes his punches on the shoulders, elbows and forearms. It is well to remember this point when you are inclined to become over-anxious and punch freely when your opponent is covered up. Two can play the same game and get the same results. If he did not hurt you when you were protected it stands to reason you are not going to inflict any damage.

Should your opponent go into a "shell," as it is called, the proper thing to do is to stand away out of range and peck away with a light jab, being on the alert however to watch for a lowering of the guard and drive in sharply with a straight right.

Against a clever opponent with a long left you can use this defense to corner him or get within striking range without too many points being scored against you. You will be able to reach him with body blows when you get in close or drive him against the ropes and then drive in with short solid blows with both hands.

Slipping the Punch

The art of "slipping a punch" is one of the lost arts. Why? Just because the boxers of today try to hit and keep hitting all the time instead of trying to make an opponent miss a blow, block it and then striking back with the same motion of the hand. Slipping a punch is difficult for the beginner and failing disconcerts the user.

Blocking a blow means that the hand used has performed its service and must be brought back to put it in position to use again to block or hit. Slipping a punch is more advantageous than blocking a punch. Your hands are always in position to strike and you get more power behind your punch because the incoming boxer adds effect to the punch. It is far better to use the hands for two purposes than confining them to one—blocking. If a punch is to be "slipped" over the shoulder, paving the way for a right counter, you step to the left about five inches, which is just about enough to permit the blow to go over your shoulder, and place you in position for a clear opening to the body. The punch can be made to pass over or to the side and you can counter with either hand as you think best. Study of an opponent's style will determine which punch may be used to the best advantage.

Slipping a punch over the left shoulder, your move is to the right about six inches, you can either hook to the body with your own left or bring it up to the jaw according to the opening left by your opponent. The left hook to the body is more effective and has more chance of landing cleaner than the hook to the head which has to curl around your opponent's arm.

Beginners are advised to use a headguard to protect the eyes and ears, and mouthpieces to guard the mouth against injury in training. But they should not take punches unnecessarily because they are so protected. It is a bad habit and one that may prove costly. Practise to block or slip punches in training is just as important with the guard, because it lessens the chance of becoming careless when boxing.

Shadow Boxing

Shadow boxing has a definite place in the training schedule as you will find out after going through what may appear from observation as meaningless and somewhat foolish motions. The actual blows, moves and actions one performs in a boxing contest are used and while performing these motions it must be realized that the loose play of the hands and feet tend to limber up the muscles and free them from constriction.

The fact that you have an imaginary foe in front of you, that you have no solid object to arrest your blows, makes it harder on the wind than actually boxing. That is when you should go through your breathing exercises and in so doing get your heart beating steadily.

It was always well to limber up three or four rounds by shadow boxing before you put on the gloves. In this way you will be able to warm up the muscles of your body, start the heart beating regularly and firmly and accustom the lungs to the exercises you are about to perform.

So many beginners, and this goes for some professionals too, mistake the importance of shadow boxing as aimless hopping and skipping around the gymnasium with no thought of deriving any benefit out of the exercise. That is not the purpose of the work at all and one would be better off if he does not do any shadow boxing at all if he enters into the motions with that thought in mind.

All exercises were devised and developed to serve certain worthwhile purposes. Shadow boxing has been proven to be a stimulating warm-up that limbers the muscles, regulates the breathing, etc. This means that you should go through the exact moves you would if there were an opponent in front of you, making sure, however, that you do not go through your motions too speedily on this account. Should you make this mistake you will soon find yourself well winded before two minutes have expired.

Assume the position "On Guard." Snap out a left jab just the way you would against a moving object. Keep the right hand in the position of blocking a blow. Snap out a jab again and step forward as you do so. Then strike out with a straight right. Bring the hands back quickly in a defensive pose. Step around as though seeking an opening. Bob your head as though to duck a blow, turn a bit to the side, raising your left slightly as though to ward off a blow and follow through with a hook. This is the act of blocking and following it up with a hook as you learned in a previous lesson. Bring your right foot up on a line with the left and lower your hands as you do so. From this crouching position let drive with both hands in the Dempsey style. It is best if you direct your blows to the body of your imaginary opponent.

Go forward slowly with mincing, short steps and punch out a tattoo with both hands. This is as though you were driving your opponent back. Halt and then back away a step or two and then charge forward with fast swinging hands as though you resumed the offensive when your opponent let up his attack. Cover up and sway from side to side. This as though you were defending yourself against a two-fisted attack to the head. As you bob and weave get your hands in punching position and level off with a hook high to the head and a straight right to the body. These moves are helpful in learning to step up your attack when taking advantage of an opening, coming out fighting from a crouch or covering up until your head clears. These pointers are something you will have to learn while concentrating on getting the best out of your exercises preliminary to actually boxing.

Another good move is to walk around the gymnasium briskly while uppercutting with both hands or rolling the shoulders so as to give full play to the muscles and shoulder blades.

You should be careful about your footwork while shadow boxing. By this is meant don't try to be fancy by executing "dance steps," jogging up and down, hopping from side to side, or making any other move you would not execute in a regular boxing bout.

Remember at all times not to form any habits that will arrest your progress or prove harmful in boxing lessons.

A Further Step in Your Boxing Lessons

Now that you have learned the fundamentals of boxing it is important that you learn how masters of the various boxing points employed each blow to particular advantage. Read carefully the points described and practise them as faithfully as you did your lessons. In this way you will be able to polish your boxing methods and improve your style both in delivering blows and guarding against them.

Champions do not win titles because they are proficient in just one or two blows. They are proficient in them all. But it so happens that the perfection of one certain blow, and the use of it at the proper time, stamped them as outstanding.

By studying the various blows as used by outstanding champions you will be able to determine the particular blow best adapted to your style. By so doing you can concentrate on perfecting it so that you will have it on tap when the opportunity presents itself for its best use. In this way champions are made and by employing the same care and hours of practise you too can become master of a finishing punch.

How to Hit Hard

AN INTERVIEW WITH JACK DEMPSEY
By Frank G. Menke, Noted Sports Editor and Authority

The golfer who rises to stardom is to one who acquires the knack of putting his BODY into his drives. The dub is the ARM SWINGER.

The greatest sluggers in baseball history were the ones who put the ENTIRE BODY into their swings. The weak hitters are those who swing with ARM POWER.

And the knockout specialists in ringdom are the men who have their WHOLE BODY concentrated on their punches.

A man need not be bulky, nor gigantic, nor amazingly strong to be a superlative driver on the links, a home run artist or a knockout specialist. The fellow who is comparatively small and light, can, by concentrated BODY POWER, OUT-SLUG THE GIANTS AT ANY GAME, provided these giants are merely arm hitters.

Bob Fitzsimmons, Kid McCoy, Stanley Ketchell, Jack Dillon, Joe Walcott, Sam Langford in their younger days were not big in stature. Walcott and Langford were hardly taller than bantamweights. Ketchell and Dillon were of average size. Fitzsimmons and McCoy were only big middleweights. Yet those two men compiled an amazing knockout total against men who were from three to twelve inches taller, and from ten to seventy-five pounds heavier.

In his best days, when Langford was knocking out all the fellows who dared to try conclusions with him, he was asked about his knockout "secret."

"T'aint no secret," Sam replied. "All ah does is put mah hips behind them punches!"

That's the knockout prescription, which, elaborated upon, reads; When you swing with your fist you should automatically swing and let the hip and body follow along with the punch.

Some years ago, while I was training for a fight, an ambitious youngster came to my camp, sparred with me one day, and afterward asked, "What are my faults?"

"The chief one," I told him, "is that you are hitting only with arm power. You can't do any real damage that way. Certainly you cannot score any knockout. The thing to do is to let go with your fist and as you do, let your whole body go with it. Make the action fast and concentrated, and with your whole body behind the punch."

"But," he said, "suppose I missed? I might spin myself all the way around the ring and I'd look like a sucker to the crowd."

The kid was right, from his viewpoint. And his way of looking at things is that "safety first" idea which percolates all through ringdom today—to the detriment of knockout results. But there is another way of looking at it—the way Bob Fitzsimmons, the Langfords, the Ketchells and other great hitters looked at it. I explained it to the youngster in this fashion:—

"Don't let go until you are reasonably sure you won't miss. And don't let your head get muddled up by the fear of what will happen if you do miss. Swing with the one thought of hitting your man and knocking him out. Swing with everything you've got to swing with. If you do miss—well, that's something that belongs to the future, and the future easily takes care of itself.

"If you are afraid to take a full body swing at a man because you might miss and "look like a sucker"—well, you'd better quit the game right now. For if you won't venture you can't gain. Babe Ruth looked like a sucker when he missed a swing but he was out there swinging just the same. And when he connected—well he still holds the home run record and that came from swinging. Fitz and those boys missed plenty but they kept right there swinging, even if they did look foolish.

"I missed a few myself. I spun around when I did and undoubtedly looked like a sucker. But I wasn't worried about missing and did not mind being laughed at. While "safety first" boys wouldn't take a chance of missing got nowhere in particular, I grabbed myself a championship."

Getting body power into a swing with a baseball bat, a golf stick or with the driving of a punch seems like a simple trick. But it isn't. The probable explanation is some sort of human willingness to risk the danger of missing and go tumbling off balance.

Nothing terrifies a human much more than to be bumped off balance. If you don't believe it, just collide with some friend and watch the wild expression on his face and his frantic effort to regain his balance. If someone else is watching he will make a pitiful effort to appear anything but silly.

Every youngster taking up boxing swings gingerly at first. The action is aim—not body action—because he won't risk going off balance if he misses. He is at the beginning, a "safety first" athlete.

In my earliest days as a ringman I was like all the others—an arm swinger. I didn't follow through with my punches. Therefore my blows lacked body power. All they carried was the strength of my arm, and you can't lull anyone to sleep with arm punches.

I knew I was doing wrong; that I wasn't getting the pile-driver force into my blows to achieve knockout success. My pals in those days knew it too. They kept coaching me. Telling me to follow through my punches with my body.

"Let the body go with the swing; swat with your hips!" they would yell at me.

I tried but I just couldn't follow through.

Then came the day when I was in the gymnasium with one of those big bags in front of me. I tried to get the BODY POWER knack but it couldn't be done. When suddenly I grasped the idea.

"If I lift my right foot off the floor, stand rigidly on my left leg, and then take a right hand swing at the bag, my body must follow through with the punch. I cannot hold it back because I am braced on my right leg."

I tried it out and that is how I got the knack of forceful body punching.

Every fellow who cannot naturally get his body into his punches can do as I did. Here is the system:

Lift the right foot off the floor and stand on the left leg. Now let go with a hard right hand punch for the bag. The body, not being braced on the right side, must follow along with the punch. You will quickly find yourself crashing FULL POWER punches into the bag.

Alternate, of course! Try right hand swings for a while. Then try left handers, lifting up the left foot and standing on the right. Very quickly you will get the old follow through idea.

Keep on doing that for a week or ten days. By that time the trick of getting the body into all your punches will be easy. After that you can go back to the business of standing on both feet and socking from that position. You won't have any real trouble getting the WHOLE BODY into the swing after that sort of practise. It will be automatic.

The trick in hard hitting isn't merely to smack a bullseye. Your purpose is to DRIVE all the way THROUGH the object that you hit the same as a golfer or a baseball slugger smacks the ball.

Don't time your blow so that its force is spent at the moment it connects. Aim your blows so that they will be at the zenith of power when they land.

Merely hitting an opponent's chin or body isn't anything remarkable. Both parts of the human frame-work can stand up under rather heavy bombardment. Your ambition, if you want to score a knockout, is to let go for the chin, or body, with the punch gaining momentum on its journey, and which, when it lands, still has enough momentum to drive THROUGH the object you strike. Don't aim merely to hit your man. AIM TO DRIVE THROUGH HIM.

When your fist collides with the jaw or body, that is the moment requiring all the "follow through" force you can generate.

If you want to become a knockout specialist, just keep these basic principles in mind.

1. Don't let go with your punches unless you are reasonably sure of hitting your target.

2. If you are swinging a right hander let the force and power start from your right and then by the "follow-through" transfer it to the left in the direction of your opponent. If you shoot a left hander, then, of course, the procedure is reversed. The power and momentum start on your left side and shifted with lightning-like rapidity to the right.

3. Don't aim to merely hit your man. Aim to drive your punch through him! That's vital for knockout success because if you pull up when you land, the damage will be slight. It isn't the impact that unsettles the other fellow; it is the terrific drive after you have landed.

The man with knockout ambitions won't get very far if he lands his punch at the end of his swing because the power will have spent itself before the blow reaches the target.

To land a punch so that the whole weight goes crashing along after the moment of impact, it is necessary to be close to your man at the moment you start your swing. Otherwise the punch won't land until the real power is spent and there is nothing left for the follow-through.

You can't land short punches unless you are willing to get in close to your man and take the chance of being belted a few yourself. Any short-range fighting that you may force, gets you near your man, and in position to knock him out, is, at the same time, risky for you. It is sometimes necessary to take those chances.

The "safety first" fighter won't go wading in and he won't take a chance. He won't try short punching because it is too risky. The man who disregards danger for a sure shot, full power punch, is the man who scores the knockouts.

Of course, there are many instances in ring history where famed sluggers went into battle and disported themselves in doleful fashion; men who never waded in at all, or who, if they did, got nowhere with their onslaughts. That is explained in two ways: (1) They found the other fellow too fast, too clever or too brainy to give them chances for knockout shots, or (2) the slugger has so much respect for the walloping power of his adversary that he wouldn't dash in and take chances with him and thus, for the time, he became a safety first boy.

An instance in the latter condition came about in New York years ago in the meeting between Jimmy McLarnin and Ray Miller. Neither let loose with the best they had in punching power. Here were two great lightweights with power-plus in their blows. It gave every indication of being one of those hit and slam the deck affairs. Each man respected the other's punching prowess too much to take a chance. Neither let loose for fear of being knocked out. So, these splendid craftsmen in the art of slugging wouldn't risk, wouldn't dare take a chance and went through ten dismal rounds with tremendous loss of prestige.

What a difference between that pair and Benny Leonard who took on sluggers like Charlie White, Ritchie Mitchell and Lew Tendler, and then, with magnificent bravery met them toe to toe and made it a survival of the man with the stoutest chin, body and heart. That is why Leonard will be remembered and glorified through the years while so many other champions will slip entirely out of even the fans' memories.

Those who espouse the cause of boxing against slugging in ringdom usually say:

"A boxer is a man who is always in position to hit and, in case he misses he is so well balanced that recovery is almost immediate. A slugger, on the other hand, puts so much violence into his drives that if he misses he is thrown off balance and therefore is not in position to take another shot until he has readjusted his whole body and resumed his stance."

Speaking as a slugger, I say that the latter idea is, in the main, very wrong. It is true that some sluggers do go whirling half way across the ring if they miss their punches. But there is an excuse for that. A man who wants to slug can remain on balance after a missed swing as easily as can a boxer.

When a slugger lets go with a right hand, the power starts on the right side. As the swing gains momentum, the power is suddenly shifted off his right leg onto his left leg. If he is smart enough to brace solidly with that left leg, then there isn't much danger of his being knocked off balance any further than the boxer.

The boxer's punches, naturally, do not carry the same violence of the body power as do the slugger's. But, as an offset, the boxer is not solidly braced on what can be called a "weight-receiving leg" as is the slugger. In almost all instances a slugger after missing a punch, can recoil into fighting position almost as rapidly as can a boxer after he has missed a punch.

Only once during my career did I pay a penalty for missing. That was the night I fought Luis Firpo.

When the gong rang I leaped at Firpo and let go with a terrific left hook. I was aiming to score a one-punch knockout. But the wallop was short. It missed the big boy's chin by an inch or two. The failure, of course, sent my body zipping violently to my right of the swing. My body wasn't exactly off balance. In fact I was rigidly braced on my right leg.

If I had been up against a fast man that night I would have made an effort to recoil quickly from the missed swing. But I didn't reckon Firpo could think or punch so fast. That was my error. For, as I was rather lazily pulling back into a new hitting position Firpo let go with his right hand, swatted me on the "button" and I felt the wallop for weeks afterward.

In my fighting days I never hoped to hit my target every time I let go. But I was always fighting in such a way, that, if I missed with one punch I would be able to throw another —and another—before my foeman could hop out of range. You don't get too many chances to sock a fellow who is clever and cautious at the same time. So it is always a smart trick to blaze away with as many chain-lightning punches as you can when you trap him into close-range battling.

Whatever success I had wasn't due to a one-punch attack. Whenever I saw an opening, or had trapped my man, I fired away with every punch at my command. I just volleyed blows into him and never stopped until he had escaped or I had dropped him to the floor.

These were the rules I followed and I think are good ones for those who wish to achieve knockout success in the prize ring.

The Left Jab as used by Jackie Fields
former World's Welterweight Champion

Not long ago the inquiring reporter of a daily newspaper stopped a crowd of youngsters at play and asked them which they would rather be, "the President of the United States or the Heavyweight Champion of the World." Surprising though it may seem a number of the youngsters prefered to be ruler of a fistic kingdom. There was something glamorous about being the champion of the world to their young minds no doubt because they were more publicized in a manner to appeal to their idea of importance and leadership.

Be that as it may the readers of these lessons are interested in boxing no doubt for the pleasure of acquainting themselves with the doings of their favorite fighters. Some like to put on the gloves for the fun of it, others to compete in the amateur ranks or adopt the game as a profession. This article is for the boy who wants to get ahead in the finest sport requiring every attribute of physical endeavor.

Jackie Fields liked the sport from the start. He had his idols in the game and when he reached the top he decided to pass on some of the points he learned to those youngsters who, like him, started from the bottom and reached the heights as a member and winner on the American Olympic team and then won a world's crown as a professional.

Let Jackie tell the story:

"The scene is laid in Los Angeles. My idol was a man much older than I, who had boxed and handled some of the greatest fighters of his time. His name was William Francis Rooney, but he was better known to the rank and file as plain "Gig."

"From the first time I came in contact with Rooney we were inseparable. He was the only man to handle my affairs and the combination worked out ideally so much so that I advise every youngster to be very careful in his selection of a manager and sticking to him after the choice is made. Faithfulness is one of the greatest and worthiest traits the game requires. The value of an understanding mentor pays big dividends to the youngster whose mind must be free of worry and a great deal depends on the care one exercises in his personal and professional dealings with everyone he comes in contact with during his career as a professional boxer.

Rooney had seen too many so-called game fellows battered to ribbons and knowing the game from all angles he taught me the fundamentals of boxing and made me stick to learning them until I had mastered the intricacies of scientific boxing before permitting me to engage in even an amateur contest.

Rooney stressed the value of the left jab. He figured once a fellow learned how to hit out straight he would seldom make the mistake of swinging and leaving openings for counter blows. The wisdom of Gig's teaching is manifest in the few real whippings I had to endure, the ease with which I won a world's amateur title and my steady rise in the professional ranks.

I used some novel methods of practise outside of the gymnasium and took my younger sister in on the scheme. Every morning I would pose in front of a mirror and Sis would turn on a phonograph record. During the three minutes or so the record played I would go through the motions of the straight left, jabbing sharply out at the reflection of my chin, bringing the hand back fast and repeat the move over and over again. I kept my hand high so that the shoulder muscles became inured to the strain and as they became strong responded to instant command. This is very important. Starting off fresh in a setto, the left hand is easily held high. As time passes one notices the strain and the left begins to droop slightly. This should not happen because your opponent watches for such a sign of weakness and snaps through a blow before you can bring up your hand to fend or ward off the blow.

"The second, or fraction of one, is all a fast boxer needs to score with a blow. You must strengthen the shoulder muscles so that the left is ready for instant use.

"I have been in retirement from professional boxing for several years. With the knowledge gained in keeping fit during my early days as a boxer I regularly perform the various exercises and find that these have been of great help in my daily life and business career. Conscientious work in the gym taught me the joys of healthful living which came about by hard painstaking work. I want to pass on a word of advice to youngsters. If you look on your work as a task to be gotten over with in a hurry don't bother to start because you will not gain anything whether you work a few minutes or an hour. You must like your work because a willing mind absorbs lessons quickly and makes what you considered tough knots easy and all the more enjoyable after you have solved them."

Jack Dempsey and the Left Hook

Probably no fighter of modern ring history could deliver the left hook with more deadly accuracy than Jack Dempsey. When it is recalled that Dempsey was strictly a "one-punch" fighter when he competed in his early days around the mining camps of Colorado and Utah and his sole punch was a swinging right, it is all the more remarkable that he perfected a different punch with the left hand and by its prolific use is acclaimed one of the greatest champions of all time. The value of the left hook as a decisive blow was clearly emphasized by the long string of knockouts Dempsey amassed on his way to the top and its use after he won the championship.

They tell a story about Dempsey having his right hand

tied to his side and forced to rely on the left alone for hours at a stretch in the gymnasium. Many sparring matches were hopelessly one-sided affairs because Dempsey had to defend himself by shifting his body to avoid blows and depend on his left to keep his opponent off or to attack. The long hours of practise and punishment brought Dempsey's "shift and roll" method into being, perfected the crouching position he was to use in later years and taught him how to get body leverage into his delivery of blows.

Dempseys method of attack was a bobbing, weaving shift of the entire body with the hands level with his hips so that when he got within striking distance he could let fly with either hand. His favored weapon was the left. Striking swiftly and upward in perfect rhythm he was able to get terrific leverage behind his blows. Perfect coordination of the eye and hand permitted Dempsey to strike without loss of motion and few misses were ever recorded against him. If Jack did miss, the weaving roll of his body placed him in the proper position to strike out with his right hand, so that if he was slightly off balance that position made him doubly dangerous.

While it is true that Dempsey was noted for his perfect timing and convincing results with blows to the jaw it would not be correct to say that he relied strictly on that point as his objective. The fact of the matter is that Dempsey could deliver a blow to the body with damaging results and the body was his favorite object of attack.

The manner of delivering the left hook as Dempsey did is to bring up the right foot almost on a line with the left. Simultaneously with this move you start the left hand in a shortened arc with an upward twist of the hip just before the blow lands. This is what is called "leg leverage" and adds considerably to the force of the blow. The added snap, bringing the weight of the body into play, results in a weightier punch than if the arm alone was used.

One of the surest signs that Dempsey could deliver a perfect blow is that his hands, smaller than the general run of heavyweights or men of his size are in as good shape today as the day he first started in the game. Dempsey was a great believer in the axiom: "Good tools make a better workman." For this reason the former champion was a stickler about the bandages he used and wound them around his precious maulies himself. Several times when Dempsey wrapped his bandages in the ring he unhurriedly took his time about wrapping them properly and the importance or impatience of the great throng did not have a bit of effect on him. He took his time and made certain that his hands were properly protected against the hard punishment they would be subjected to after the bell sounded for the first round. Heavy bandages, heavy flannel or felt, were his favorite when punching the heavy bag or in sparring sessions.

This is a good point of advice for the beginner. Before attempting to subject the hands to the unusual strain of battering them against a heavy object it is well to see that they are properly bandaged. This will relieve the strain of steady pounding and lessen the chances of dislocations and jarring the small bones of the hands.

This is very important, as you will soon find out, after a few sessions at the bags or in sparring sessions.

There are many cases when the jab and the hook can be used in combination. As you progress in your boxing you will readily detect openings, or chances, to use the hook or jab, or both in combination.

The Combination Left Jab and Left Hook as used by Jack Britton

Jack Britton, former welterweight champion of the world, was the possessor of a combination left jab and left hook that was a beauty to watch and disastrous to the many rivals of his crown. The weight of the combined blows permitted Britton to carry on in the ring against first rate foemen many years after men who had started in the game with him had hung up their gloves and went into retirement. Britton continued in his chosen profession several years after he passed the forty mark.

Britton was a master at jabbing. Oftentimes Jack noticed an opponent was tipped off balance with a jab and the smartness of the veteran was noticeable as he took advantage of the opening. Without the loss of the fraction of a second Britton would follow through with a cutting left hook.

Britton did not confine his combination blow to the head alone. Using his head and thinking every second he was in action Jack would unexpectedly shift his attack to the body to the chagrin and dismay of an opponent who might have been set to block a punch to the jaw.

That is the purpose of the two blows in combination with each other. It is ridiculous to think that you can use both blows while standing off at long range against an opponent considered good enough to match his skill against your own.

There is a time and place for every blow. Unless you can outwit the other fellow, fool him into thinking you are going to use a certain blow and then cross him by employing a different one, there is no use of learning a variety of blows. Mixing up the different blows is the real science of boxing and comes under the heading of ring generalship. The fact that one fighter can do a thing better than another proves the superiority he holds over a rival and results in the needed margin for victory.

That is the reason that practise, and plenty of it, is urged in your boxing lessons.

Britton was a smart boxer, probably one of the greatest the game has ever known. Diligent practise and study made him the master ringman of his time and is often mentioned when smart boxers of the game are discussed.

Jack's method of delivering the combination left jab and left hook is a good one to practise. Standing straight up, Britton pawed out with his left and watched with keen eye for a bare let-up or sign of carelessness on the part of his opponent. Noting this, Britton would lance through with a jab and drawing back slightly would crook his arm at the elbow and follow through with a hooking glove to the jaw. The same method would be employed successfully to the body. A feint or a light jab to the body would act as a leader for the heavier, more punishing hook to the same place.

The blow, or combination of blows, requires long practise on the heavy bag. The chances of striking the thumb against the heavy bag are great for the beginner. Hooking into the bag calls for perfect timing so that the face of the knuckles strikes the bag evenly. It is far better to strike a soft object that gives like a training bag than to hit the solid object like the head or jaw until you have learned how to hook properly. A sore knuckle resulting from improper delivery of the blow on the soft bag is warning that you are delivering the blow improperly. The same improper delivery in a bout might result in a broken knuckle or hand.

Unless you are able to master the art of proper hitting you will strike with the thumb or first knuckle with greater force. You must practise to ensure against breakage of the hands or spraining your wrist.

Gene Tunney's Right Cross

Gene Tunney was noted for his straight punching. Tunney was one fighter who rarely made mistakes. Swinging is a cardinal mistake in boxing, and since Tunney made a thorough study of the art of hitting, he never fell into error by swinging his blows. Tunney directed and propelled all punches straight from the shoulder.

The fact that Tunney ascended the highest rung on pugilism's ladder by reason of resounding victories over the best men in his class attests the value of straight hitting. Whether it was jabbing with the left or hitting with the right, all Gene's blows were driven on a straight line and rarely missed their mark.

Gene's manner of delivering the right cross was the most perfect blow in his repertoire. His blows were not always directed to the jaw or chin. Tunney was considered the greatest right-hand-puncher-to-the-body in the history of the game. The effect of this blow was not always apparent to the spectator as the blow, a short one, was generally driven while at close quarters. This type of blow is not spectacular from a ringsider's point of view and sometimes passes unnoticed by all but the receiver. The fact that Gene was able to weaken heavier, sturdier opponents with these blows and then step away and jab with little returns, speaks well for the power of the short right to the body.

Those who saw the first Tunney-Dempsey fight will remember the blow with which Gene started the battle. It was a straight right direct from the shoulder. It landed high and grazed Dempsey's cheek. Many experts thought the blow would have scored a clean knockout had it landed one inch lower. In the return meeting at Chicago it was a right to the jaw that spilled Dempsey in the eighth round.

Gene's two victories over Jack Dempsey and other noteworthy performances on his climb to the top were achieved by proficient use of straight blows, either left jabs or right crosses. Gene got plenty of power into his punches because he knew the secret of meeting head-long rushes with firm fists and used the force behind straight blows to pile up points.

In training Tunney devoted considerable time to the heavy bag. Most of his blows were directed near the bottom of the bag proving that Gene realized the punishing effect of a body blow and the weakening process blows of that type inflicted on an opponent.

Gene used to pace off from the bag, take his proper position on guard and then strike out forcefully. A short step forward with the right foot as he delivered the blow added force to the power of the blow.

It is best to practise this punch as frequently as possible. This is the best blow to finish off an opponent or weaken him to the extent of making him lower his guard and permit a straight shot to the jaw. While it is true that a right to the body leaves you open to some extent for a left hook, you must remember the best effect to be gained by this blow, with less chance of getting hit a counter blow, is to wait until you are in close and then drive for the short ribs or region of the heart.

One of the best reasons advocated for the use of the straight right is that the shoulder is parallel with the jaw making it a natural guard against a hook or swing.

Tony Canzoneri and the One-Two

Tony Canzoneri, one of the few champions to win three world's titles, was a finished artist in the use of a wide assortment of blows. Tony's right to fame however was achieved by the perfect use of the difficult combination of punches known as the one-two punch.

Canzoneri boxed on the style of the old timers who were adept at slipping punches. His keen eye for distance and his ability to gauge the precise moment to snap in his blows had a devastating effect on his rivals. Instead of bringing up his hands to ward off a blow Tony turned his shoulder and in so doing allowed the punch to miss the target and left the opening he calculated on. In this way he was able to slide into range and put over the "double punch," the short left jab and follow-through right cross. A careless lead, a slight turn of the head and Canzoneri brought his famed punch into play. Both of the blows as delivered by the great champion were the straight variety and followed each other so rapidly that they seemed like one blow delivered with the same hand. That is the secret of the one-two punch.

If you jab out and fail to follow up with a right cross your opponent will be able to bring his own left hand up to guard or cross with his right before you can score with your right and this counter blow will be heavy because you will have furnished momentum for the punch.

Don't attempt to use the one-two punch while going away. It will be wasted effort. The effectiveness of the blow depends on the added power you get behind your forward moving body and as the blows should be of the short variety it can be seen that by going away you have destroyed the technique of the two punches. It is difficult enough to land one blow while going away. It is plain to see that attempting to land two blows in rapid order is much more difficult.

Lou Nova and the Right or Left Uppercut

Lou Nova is a splendid boxer for a big man. His earlier fights, upward through the amateur ranks, were won by the speed he displayed on his well formed legs and delivery of blows. Nova's mastery of the right and left uppercuts have often been pointed out as the reason for his high standing in the game. The effectiveness of these blows were amply demonstrated in Lou's winning fights against outstanding contenders for the world's heavyweight crown.

That these blows were to pave the way for Nova's high ranking was noted when the California heavyweight forsook the amateur ranks and started out as a professional. Nova took what many considered unnecessary punches to get in close and whip a right or left uppercut to the jaw. He persevered in the use of these blows despite punishment and as he mastered the blows it was seen that he was scoring heavily with them and fended off punches that formerly arrested his charges.

Nova steps in fast carrying the fight to his opponent. He carries his hands high. This causes his shoulders to lift so that natural protection afforded by the hunched shoulders protects the jaw. As he gets within range he uppercuts with either hand, sometimes to the head but mostly to the body. With this as a starter Lou switches his attack by looping sharp overhand punches and these carry plenty of power because he gets added lift behind the blows.

Nova keeps his elbows close to his body as he delivers the uppercut. This means that he gets the most out of the punch because he is not exposed and his opponent cannot hit him or get his hands inside of his arms and spread them or lean against them and nullify their hitting-out power. Taking the swing out of his punches would result in forcing a rival to push, and, as everyone knows, there is no real force behind a pushing or shoving blow. This is a good point to remember. Try to keep your elbows close to your body. The elbows make an effective guard and this will enable you to ward off many punches. Another thing, it means that your uppercuts will naturally be straight blows and have less distance to travel thus making them more certain of hitting the mark with the minimum time and distance needed to execute the blow.

Unless your opponent is spent and has his head down, the uppercut cannot be rightly termed a knockout blow. It is a jarring punch and most effective when delivered at close range. Forcing the head of your opponent back with an uppercut permits you to hook with either hand, as the case may be, and in most cases as Nova uses it, the following punch may be the decisive one of the contest.

How to Second a Boxer

You must hold the fighter's confidence and respect. This feeling must be mutual otherwise you may not obtain satisfactory results.

The personal attitudes of a fighter and his second must be sympathetic because without it a fighter is apt to disregard advice, use his own judgment and in most instances be faulty. The second, on the other hand, is in a position to observe both boys, and more often detect weakness or faulty execution of blows and defense.

If a fighter doesn't respect your judgment, your time and efforts are wasted.

The main attribute of a second is calmness. He must be calm, collected and in full possession of his wits at all times. Speaking calmly with deliberation often quiets the unstrung nerves of the fighter who has been through a tempestuous round. This psychological effect cannot be overemphasized. The fans are stamping their feet and shouting. The house is in an uproar that is bound to affect the fighter and he returns to his corner bewildered. It is then that the calmness of the second is transmitted to the excited brain of the boy as a soothing restorative.

You must have a complete knowledge of First Aid. You must know how to treat wounds, a bruise or bleeding nose because it is very important that the fighter is not further handicapped by distorted vision, due to blood pouring from an eye wound or that his throat is choked with blood from a lip or mouth wound. Above all you must be sanitary. Use only clean towels, clean cotton and a fresh sponge to douse the fighter's head. Never sponge the mouth of your fighter. Give him a swallow of fresh water out of a bottle and have him spit into the bucket instead of permitting him to let it pour over his body.

You must have your medical kit on hand, the instant you note that an injury has been sustained so that no time is lost when the boy returns to his corner.

You have but a minute between rounds and sometimes it may be necessary to act on the spur of the moment. This may not turn out to be the proper course and then again it will in a measure be more helpful than if you were to become excited and do nothing. For this reason you are expected to train yourself for emergency treatments so that the percentage of errors is reduced to a minimum.

Don't talk too much to your fighter; you are not only wasting your time but annoy him exceedingly. He knows what he is about and is keyed to a high pitch. In a few words inform him what you have observed and whatever suggestions you have to make. Many times there is nothing to say because your fighter is following pre-battle plans and they are working out smoothly. A small pat on the arm or on an encouraging word is sufficient.

One of the worst things you can do is warn your boy about his opponent's hitting power. Explain to him how to move around or raise an arm to neutralize that power. In this way you do not emphasize the fact that his opponent is the harder hitter. Otherwise no matter how courageous the fighter is you will instil in him a fear which may become magnified should a telling blow be delivered.

The first thing to do at the close of each round is to go to work on your charge. Take a clean towel and rub it over his face. Don't urge him to drink, offer him the bottle and if he wants it he will open his mouth. Then give it to him. Place your fingers in the waistband of his tights and hold it out so that he may breath more freely. Instruct him to relax while he is in his corner so that his throbbing muscles and pulsing heart may return to normal so much easier. Massage his biceps and if he appears leg weary, rub the calves of his legs.

These rules do not always apply to all boxers. They are not machines. Human feelings and mental processes differ. This means you must use good judgment in the treatment of the boy you handle so that the best results will be obtained.

Some fighters are spirited and often take unnecessary chances. You must give him enough encouragement so that he will feel you are sympathetic and at the same time retain enough discipline over him to keep him in hand.

Others are more reserved and work smoother and better under frequent words of encouragement.

There are times when you have to joke with a fighter who for some reason or other is in a solemn mood. Kidding him often brings him out of the "dumps" and he assumes a brighter outlook as he goes out for the succeeding round.

Knowing the moods of your fighter is as important as your knowledge of the game otherwise you cannot accomplish the same results. Your knowledge of the game combined with your ability to smooth the mental processes of the fighter is the ideal combination of the successful second.

Important notes before a fight:

Check over the equipment; make sure that you have everything before you are called to enter the ring.

Play fair! Observe the rules of the commission as to the quantity of soft bandage and adhesive tape permitted.

Examine the hands of your boy's opponent in order that they enter the ring equal in that respect.

Do not jerk or tug at the hands of your charge when you put on the gloves. Take it easy and lace them properly; make secure knots and then cut off the metal tips.

After the fighters are called to the center of the ring for instructions, have the referee examine the body of your boy to show it is not greased. You have no right to touch the other boy. That is the job of the referee. He will examine the other boy if you so request, which is proper under the rules.

It is true that most referees give the same instructions—but you must not appear to know it all, and do not show any disrespect. Listen carefully and have your fighter do the same because under the interpretation of some Commissions the rules may vary somewhat and the change is worth knowing before your boy is penalized. You must be attentive at all times because ignorance of any rule is inexcusable.

You have the right to call the referee's attention to any

infraction of the rules on the part of your boy's opponent. He is not infallible and will listen to your complaint provided you express yourself properly and there is justification for the complaint. Don't shout or berate him. Be calm, speak slowly and in that way gain your point because he will realize you are not trying to trick him by exaggerating a minor offense.

Whatever you do, make your fighter take all the time he is permitted when he is knocked down. Playing to the gallery and getting up without taking a count just to show off that he is not hurt is not only bad business but often results in obsorbing unnecessary punishment. The knockdown, whether it is for 3 or 9 seconds, counts, just the same in the scoring. The additional six seconds rest may be the margin between victory and defeat. So impress upon the fighter that he should watch your signals so that he will know what to do and take full advantage of the rest permitted him under the rules.

How to Judge Fights Correctly

How do you judge a boxing contest?

Does your decision tally with that of the judges, or are you a member of the always present minority who boo the decision of the official judges? Maybe these pointers will help you out and put you aboard the bandwagon of those who agree with the judges and know what it is all about.

In judging a contest you should bear these points in mind.
1. Clean hitting.
2. Aggressiveness.
3. Cleverness.
4. Fouls.
5. Knockdowns.

Make out a score card so that you can put down your points and the winner of the rounds as you go along and base your judgment on these grounds:

AGGRESSIVENESS: So many mistake aggressiveness to mean tearing in to attack regardless of the amount of blows and punishment inflicted by his opponent. That is not aggressiveness. That is determination. Unless the contestant employing such methods is able to break through his opponent's guard and inflict punishment, rushing of this sort is scored against him. Aggressiveness is a steady forcing of an opponent, making him break away, cover up to stand to and swap punches, and scoring the greater number of clean hits. Or when contestants of the "fighter" and "boxer" type get together, the fighter invariably disdains to stand off and box. Instead he will press his man until he gets him to stand still and slug. If the fighter" is able to worst the "boxer" he gets credit for that as aggressiveness and ring generalship.

CLEVERNESS: This does not mean running away from an opponent or speed afoot necessarily. Warding off a lead, beating him to the punch, neutralizing the other man's natural style of fighting and making him fight at a disadvantage by making him slug or box, as the case may be; effective guarding in the clinches and clean counter blows. These all come under the general heading of cleverness.

FOULS: This takes in low punches, illegal blows such as the kidney punch, rabbit punch, hitting with the palm or wrist of the glove, rubbing the palm of the glove across an opponent's face, holding in the clinches, unnecessary roughness, butting, hitting before an opponent has regained his feet or falling to the floor after a knockdown without being hit to avoid punishment. If low blows are struck unintentionally and the referee permits the contest to continue it is well to judge how much the illegal blow has weakened the boxer stricken and if it has prevented him from doing his best. If your judgment is that the referee erred in permitting the contest to continue under such a handicap it is only fair to make due allowance and so judge the remainder of the round.

Deliberate holding in the clinches is a foul and should be so scored. Fouls, whether deliberate or otherwise, count more than a knockdown in the opinion of capable judges. This is fair. A boxer cannot be expected to do his best if incapacitated through no fault of his own. Many illegal punches escape the eyes of the referee. If a contestant continues to use illegal tactics, and is not detected by the referee, it is up to the judges to notify that official.

KNOCKDOWNS: This is a point on which many judges disagree. The value of a knockdown is a matter of opinion. How badly is a boxer hurt? Was it "one" blow that sent him down or a series of blows and how long did he stay down? A clean punch, of course, counts more than a series of blows. A man may be down for 9 and still not be hurt. A good fighter will always take advantage of the full count permitted him and clear his head before resuming the contest. If a man is knocked down, takes the count and comes back to outscore his opponent by clean punching it stands to reason that the knockdown does not count for much. A knockdown to be really scored heavily should consist of a clean punch that stuns a boxer, or a series of punches that cause the same effect, and renders him easy for a follow-up attack should he get up before the full count.

Boxing Rules List 13 Fouls

There are thirteen reasons why a boxer can be disqualified by the referee who is given discretionary power to inflict penalties.
1. Hitting below the belt.
2. Hitting an opponent while he is down, or who is getting up after being down.
3. Holding an opponent or deliberately maintaining a clinch.
4. Holding with one hand and hitting with the other.
5. Butting with the head or shoulders, or hitting with the knee.
6. Hitting with the inside, or butt of the hand, wrist or elbow.
7. Hitting or "flicking" with the open glove.
8. Wrestling or roughing on the ropes.
9. Purposely going down without being hit.
10. Striking deliberately at that part of the body over the kidneys.
11. Using the pivot or rabbit punch.
12. Using abusive or profane language.
13. Failure to obey the referee after due warning.

Marquis of Queensberry Rules

1. To be a stand-up boxing match in a twenty four foot ring, or as near that size as practicable.
2. No wrestling or hugging allowed.
3. The rounds to be of three minutes' duration, and one minute rest between rounds.
4. If either man fall through weakness or otherwise, he must get up unassisted, ten seconds to be allowed him to do so, the other man meanwhile to return to his corner, and when the fallen man is on his legs the round is to be resumed and continue until three minutes have expired.

If one man fails to come to scratch in the ten seconds allowed it shall be in the power of the referee to give the award in favor of the other man.

5. A man hanging on the ropes in a helpless state, with his toes off the ground shall be considered down.

6. No seconds or any other persons to be allowed in the ring during the rounds.

7. Should the contest be stopped by any unavoidable interference, the referee shall name the time and place as soon as possible for finishing the contest, so that the match must be won or lost, unless the backers of both men agree to draw the stakes.

8. The gloves to be fair sized boxing gloves of the very best quality, and new.

9. Should a glove burst, or come off, it must be replaced to the referee's satisfaction.

10. A man on one knee is considered down, and if struck, is entitled to the stakes.

11. No shoe or boots with springs allowed.

12. The contest in all other respects to be governed by revised rules of the London Prize Ring.

The rules, as later revised, are as follows:

1. All contests to be decided in a roped ring, not less than 16 feet nor more than 24 feet square.

2. Contestants to box in light boots or shoes, (without spikes) or in socks.

3. In all contests the number and duration of rounds must be specified. The limit of rounds shall be 20 three minute rounds; the interval between rounds shall be one minute. All championship contests shall be of 20 three minute rounds. The gloves to be of minimum weight 6 ounces and shall be provided by the promoter.

4. The contestants shall be entitled to the assistance of not more than four seconds, who are to be approved by the promoter; and no advice can be given by seconds during the progress of a round.

5. In all contests the decision shall be given in favor of the contestant who attains the greatest number of points. The points shall be for—Attack: Direct, clean hits with the knuckle part of the glove on any part of the front or sides of the head or body above the belt. Defense: Guarding, slipping, ducking or getting away.

Where points are otherwise equal, the preference shall

be given to the contestant who does most of the leading off, or displays the best style.

6. The referee may disqualify a contestant for delivering a foul blow intentionally or otherwise, for holding, butting, palming, shouldering, falling without receiving a blow, wrestling, or for boxing unfairly by hitting with the open glove, with the wrist or elbow, or for roughing.

7. If, in the opinion of the referee, a deliberate foul is committed by a contestant such a contestant shall not be entitled to a prize.

8. The referee shall have the power to stop a contest, if, in his opinion, a man is unfit to continue, and that man shall be deemed to have lost the contest.

9. No seconds or other person shall be allowed in the ring during the rounds. Each contestant shall be entitled to the assistance of not more than four seconds, and must take up their position outside of the ring, and who must not, under pain of disqualification of their principal by the referee, coach, assist in any manner, or advise their principal during the rounds or enter the ring during the process of a contest. A second refusing to obey the orders of the referee shall be removed from his position and replaced by another approved by the referee.

10. The contestant failing to come up when time is called, or refusing to obey the referee, shall lose the contest. A man on one knee, or when on the ropes with both feet off the floor, shall be considered down.

11. If a contestant slips down he must get up immediately. His opponent must stand back out of distance until the fallen man is on his feet, when the contest shall be resumed. A contestant who has knocked down his opponent must immediately walk to his corner, but should the fallen man be knocked down in that corner, the contestant delivering the knockdown shall retire to the farthest corner. A man knocked down must rise unassisted in ten seconds or lose the contest.

12. Should a glove burst or come off, it must be replaced immediately to the satisfaction of the referee. The time thus lost shall be considered as no part of the stipulated period of the round.

13. The contestants shall not hit while in a clinch. A clinch shall be constituted by both men holding, either with one or both hands.

14. The referee shall decide—(1) Any question not provided in these rules; (2) The interpretation of these rules.

A Selection Of Classic Instructive Titles Relating To The
Art Of Pugilism & Self Defence
In Both War & Peace
Find our entire selection @ naval-military-press.com

ALL-IN FIGHTING
The distilled knowledge of W.E. Fairbairn, legendary SOE instructor in unarmed combat, and inventor of the Sykes-Fairbairn knife, who learned his deadly skills in 30 years on the Shanghai waterfront. Fully illustrated.
9781847348531

ART OF BOXING AND SCIENCE OF SELF DEFENCE
Former Lightweight Champion Billy Edwards shares the techniques and strategies of the sweet science in his beautifully illustrated boxing guide. Explore boxing's transition from bare knuckle spectacle to today's Marquis of Queensbury ruleset.
9781474539548

SELF DEFENCE OR THE ART OF BOXING
Ned Donnelly was a pioneer of boxing training during the late Victorian era. Explore the strategies and techniques used by this trainer of champions via a series of easy-to-follow illustrations and clear, concise coaching steps.
9781474539562

JACK GOODWIN'S BOXING

This 1920's boxing masterpiece by Jack Goodwin puts you in the shoes of a coach in that era. Uncover the best ways to run, manage and train boxers as taught by Jack Goodwin, a champion and trainer of champions in the noble science.

9781474539586

ART OF WRESTLING

George de Relwyskow Army Gymnastic Staff

In the appreciation to this book Captain Daniels, V.C., M.C., Rifle Brigade, states: "In adding a word to this book on the style of wrestling as taught at the Headquarters Gymnasium of the British Army, and having had personal experience in the various holds and throws taught, I consider it has been of great value in the training of the soldier, and the bringing out of those qualities of grit and determination which have been seen in all ranks who have taken an active part throughout the greatest war in history." 1919.

9781783313563

THE COMPLETE BOXER

Gunner Moir provides detailed instructions on the techniques he deployed to become British Heavyweight Champion. Taught in a series of easy to learn techniques, combinations, and boxing strategies.

9781474539609

KILL OR GET KILLED

Rex Applegate's "kill or be killed" helped prepare America's marines, soldiers, sailors, spies and airmen for the realities of war. This highly shared and respected work provides all you need to know about unarmed combat and close quarter engagement with the enemy.

9781474539661

BOXING (V-Five)

The Aviation Training Office of the Chief of Naval Operations

The game-changing V-Five suite of training manuals helped get a generation of American aviators fit for war. Here we explore how the airmen of the US navy trained in boxing as part of their military fitness regime.

9781474539623

THE TEXTBOOK OF WRESTLING

Get your wrestling skills matt-ready from wrestling champion and world-renown trainer Ernest Gruhn. Replete with detailed holds, throws, pins and strategies for success in a wide range of wrestling rulesets.

9781474539647

MANUAL OF PHYSICAL TRAINING 1914

(United States Army)

Published just prior to the outbreak of World War 1, this beautifully illustrated guide was designed to revolutionise the combat fitness and readiness of the US Army covering a wide range of gymnastic and combat calisthenic exercises.

9781474539708

DEAL THE FIRST DEADLY BLOW
United States Department of the Army

This Vietnam-era classic showcases in detail how the US Forces trained in close quarter combat. Known as the "encyclopaedia of combat" it helped a generation learn how to become devastating effective with empty hands, knives and bayonets alike.

9781474539722

HAND-TO-HAND COMBAT
Bureau of Aeronautics U.S Navy 1943

This is one of the best combative manuals from World War 2, developed by the US Navy V-Five Staff, that included the renowned American wrestler Wesley Brown. It is then not especially surprising that wrestling skills predominate in this manual, and form the base skill-set for this combative system.

9781474537391

ABWEHR ENGLISCHER GANGSTER METHODEN DEFENSE OF ENGLISH GANGSTERS METHODS – SILENT KILLING – FULL ENGLISH TRANSLATION

In 1942 the Wehrmacht published a training manual with the goal of countering the "silent killing" tactics used by the British commando units. The manual was – much in line with typical National Socialist terminology –titled

"Abwehr Englischer Gangster-methoden" or "Defence Against English Gangster methods".

This book was compiled due the Wehrmacht intelligence operatives uncovering of a British hand-to-hand course for the SOE, Commandos, et al, on methods of quick and silent killing (undoubtedly developed by W. E. Fairbairn and E. A. Sykes). They correctly assessed that their troops in general and particularly the Geheime Staatspolizei (Gestapo), Sicherheitsdienst (SD), their security guards, and sentries would be in grave danger when confronted by men trained in these methods. This manual/program was the Wehrmacht's response.

9781474538336

HAND TO HAND COMBAT

Francois d'Eliscu taught thousands of U.S. Army Rangers how to fight down and dirty in World War II. d'Eliscu doesn't get the press that Fairbairn and Applegate do, but he did a commendable job writing this book. It is basic, meant for training raw recruits in a short amount of time before sending them to the front, but simple is good when you are in combat, as most combative experts' will tell you.

9781474535823

WE Fairbairn's Complete Compendium of Lethal, Unarmed, Hand-to-Hand Combat Methods and Fighting In Colour

All 844 images of Fairbairn and his assistants can now for the first time be seen in full colour, lending a clarity to the practical methods of mastering the manner of dealing with an assailant, both in time of war and when placed in difficulty during unpleasant modern urban situations. These various holds, trips, kicks, blows etc. allow the average man or woman a position of security against almost any form of armed or unarmed attack.

Captain W.E. Fairbairn would have approved of this new colour version, that gives an illustrative clarity to the original that was lacking in previous monochrome reprints of his work.

All six of W.E. Fairbairn's works in one binding to create the ultimate colour compendium: Get Tough-All-In Fighting-Shooting to Live-Scientific Self-Defence-Hands Off!-Defend

9781783318735

BOXING FOR BOYS
Regtl. Sergt.-Major & B Dent Army Gymnastic Headquarters

A successful system of boxing instruction for large classes, to allow tuition with no detriment to the "backward or shy pupil". Covers Kit-On, Guard-Sparring-Advance-Point & Mark-Ducking-Medicine, Bag-Left & Right Hooks etc. The author considered that boxing systematically taught to the youth was beneficial exercise, and would have a marked elevating influence on the national character.

9781783314607

HAND-TO-HAND FIGHTING
A System Of Personal Defence For The Soldier (1918)

A tough book on the art of hand to hand fighting in the trenches of the Great War. Demonstrating techniques utilised to "do away with the enemy", many of which are barred in clean wrestling, the book includes good clear photographic illustrations presenting important attack methods including the "Hammer Lock", "Kidney Kick", "Head Twist", "Knee Groin Kick", and the "Knee Break", all very important in a man to man, life or death encounter, when fighting in the mud of the trenches.

9781783313983

COLD STEEL

A cold-war combatives classic. John Styers, US Marine and WW2 veteran, lays out his approach to close quarters combat with rifle, bayonet, stick, knife and empty hands. Explore what helped wartime and post-war Marines stay ahead of the competition with lucid imagery and clear combative descriptions.

9781474540643

THE COMPLETE KANO JIU-JITSU

Join world-famous physical culture expert H. Irving Hancock, and Jiu-Jitsu specialist Katsukama Higashi as they showcase the art of 'Kano Jiu-Jitsu' now known as Judo. Get an exclusive glimpse into the transitional era of the martial art, alongside how it uses Japanese physical culture methodologies for self-improvement.

9781474540735

SCIENTIFIC UNARMED COMBAT
The Art of Dynamic Self-Defence

Learn the esoteric Sri Lankan art of 'Cheena-Adi' with R. A Vairamuttu. This guide explores armed and unarmed self-defence drawing heavily from Indian martial culture, alongside wellness and development from Indian physical culture, fitness, diet and medicine.

9781474540728

SELF DEFENCE FOR WOMEN
COMBATO

Join the Canadian combatives legend William "Bill" Underwood as he showcases self-defence for women. Over the course of clear photography, sketches and instructions he lays out a curriculum for self-defence for the attacks women would be most likely to face.

9781474540711

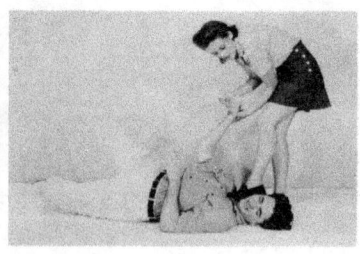

THE NEW SCIENCE
Weaponless Defence

Join wrestling champions Prof F. S Lewis, William V Gregory and Boxing Champ Tommy Burns as they showcase street orientated self-defence from people with a proven track record of fighting success. This 1906 manual via a series of photos and instructions lays out simple, tried and tested ways to keep yourself safe.

9781474540704

COMBAT CONDITIONING MANUAL
Jiu-Jitsu Defence, Bayonet Defence and Club Defence

This 1942 guide for marines lays out the basics of combat Ju Jitsu as part of an overall training regimen for US Marines. It's a holistic guide that covers defences against armed and unarmed attackers, physical fitness and even first aid.

9781474540698

BOXING TAUGHT THROUGH "SLOW MOTION FILM"

Learn the ropes from the best fighters of the 1900s-1930s in this unique boxing manual. Using stills from super slow-mo fight footage, this treasure trove unpacks the skills, tips and tactics of the champs for you to emulate at home.

9781474540681

HOW TO BOX CORRECTLY

Explore the art of boxing according to famous Bronx boxing brand Ben Lee in this 1944 how-to guide. Learn the ropes from one of the nation's top trainers and boxing journalists John J. Romano, in this warmly illustrated guide to the sweet science.

9781474540674

www.ingramcontent.com/pod-product-compliance
Lightning Source LLC
LaVergne TN
LVHW051156080426
835508LV00021B/2667